CHRIST
OF THE
REVELATION

CHRIST
OF THE
REVELATION

His Message to the Church and the World

by

J. R. Zurcher

Translated by E. E. White

Southern Publishing Association, Nashville, Tennessee

Copyright © 1980 by
Southern Publishing Association

This book was
Edited by Richard W. Coffen
Designed by Mark O'Connor

Type set: 10/11 Palatino

Printed in U.S.A.

Library of Congress Cataloging in Publication Data

Zurcher, Jean.
    Christ of the Revelation.

    1. Bible. N.T. Revelation—Criticism, interpretation, etc.
2. Jesus Christ—Person and offices.
I Title.
BS2825.2.Z8713   228'.06   79-25135
ISBN 0-8127-0261-1

Contents

Introduction

Whenever the world passes through a grave crisis, as at the present time, believers naturally turn to the prophetic word for help in understanding the significance of their times. This is undoubtedly why Christians today are showing a renewed interest in that prophetic book par excellence, the Book of Revelation.

In the past, theologians were too often the first to claim that Revelation was a sealed book, whereas the Lord specifically said to John: "Seal not the sayings of the prophecy of this book" (22:10). And today even those who consider it divinely inspired generally look upon it as a mysterious book, containing "as many mysteries as words," as Jerome, the famous translator of the Vulgate, affirmed long ago.

It is not at all surprising, therefore, that Christians have generally turned away from the prophetic word, particularly Revelation, because they have concluded that its mysteries cannot be explained. This opinion also is reflected in the meaning twentieth-century man has given to the word *apocalypse*. People commonly use *apocalyptic* to describe a period filled with extraordinary, catastrophic events. In certain languages, such as French, the word currently denotes something difficult to understand or simply describes an author's obscure style. In actual fact the word signifies just the opposite: a revelation.

No one will deny that the Book of Revelation contains mysteries. But why such puzzling language? The culture of the time and the prevailing literary customs partly justify this use of symbolic language. There are also pedagogic considerations to be taken into account. But the real reasons are of a practical nature, not to mention political. The Book of Revelation would never have come down to us today if it had been written in plain language, understandable by all. The Roman emperors first of all, and following them all the antichrists that are denounced by the prophecy, would have doomed the "seditious book" to the flames—written as it was by a man whom the highest tribunal of the empire had condemned.

The best explanation is given by Jesus Himself in reply to the disciples' question, "Why speakest thou unto them in parables?" "Because it is given unto you to know the mysteries of the kingdom of heaven, but to them it is not given" (Matthew 13:11). In other words, for His disciples the parables were intended to be a revelation of divine mysteries, whereas for the scribes and Pharisees, as well as for the enemies of Christ, they were intended to remain mysteries. "Therefore speak I to them in parables: because they seeing see not; and hearing they hear not, neither do they understand" (verse 13).

"Let none think, because they cannot explain the meaning of every symbol in the Revelation, that it is useless for them to search this book in an effort to know the meaning of the truth it contains. The One who revealed these mysteries to John will give to the diligent searcher for truth a foretaste of heavenly things. Those whose hearts are open to the reception of truth will be enabled to understand its teachings, and will be granted the blessing promised to those who 'hear the words of this prophecy, and keep those things which are written therein' " (Ellen G. White, *The Acts of the Apostles,* pp. 584, 585).

Chapter 1

A Revelation of Jesus Christ

The first three Greek words in the Book of Revelation bring us straight to the heart of the matter. They lead directly to the main theme of the book, stating clearly what it is intended to be: "The Revelation of Jesus Christ." There is no need, therefore, to look for anyone in Revelation but Jesus Christ; no need to search for anything else but the testimony of Jesus.

"A revelation": such is the actual meaning of the word *apocalypse*. In other words it is an uncovering or a disclosure. The writers of the New Testament employ the expression eighteen times. It refers either to the revelation of divine secrets (Romans 16:25; Ephesians 1:17; 1 Corinthians 14:6, 26) or to the glorious manifestation of Christ and the saved on the day of the restoration of all things (2 Thessalonians 1:7; Romans 8:19, and others).

True, the translators differ on the meaning of the opening declaration of the Book of Revelation. Some think that Jesus Christ is being designated as the *author* of the revelation. They therefore translate: "This is a revelation from Jesus Christ" (Knox translation; Phillips'), or "a revelation made by Jesus Christ" (American translation), or more explicitly, "This is the revelation given by God to Jesus Christ" (NEB). Others, considering that Jesus is the subject of the revelation, give the following translation: "The Revelation of Jesus Christ" (KJV, RSV, 20th Century).

According to the Greek text, both interpretations are grammatically correct. Nevertheless, the immediate context confirms the first interpretation rather than the second, because it is the revelation "which God gave unto him, to shew unto his servants things which must shortly come to pass" (1:1).

In actual fact, in the book, Jesus Christ is both the author and the subject of the revelation. Christ gives the revelation and announces the prophecy. It comes to Him directly from God, whose faithful and true witness He is. However, in the overall context of the book, Jesus Christ is also the subject of the revelation. Here, as elsewhere in the Scriptures, the Spirit of God bears witness to Jesus Christ—no longer He who came in the flesh and was crucified, but He who was raised from the dead, who ascended to heaven and sat down at the right hand of God's throne, who lives forever and ever, and who will return on the clouds of heaven. Jesus is truly the central figure of the whole book and the main subject of each of the visions.

John did not yet know this Jesus Christ, and we would not know Him either had He not revealed Himself in person to the prophet on Patmos. True, the Old Testament prophets, while they foretold "the sufferings of Christ," also gave an indication of "the glory that should follow" (1 Peter 1:10, 11). On the mount, Peter, James, and John saw Jesus transfigured for a moment, His face shining "as the sun" and His clothes dazzling "as the light" (Matthew 17:2). More than this, all His disciples saw Him in His resurrected form. But the "Stranger" who journeyed with the two on the road to Emmaus, like the One who addressed the disciples by the sea of Tiberias, still bore the appearance of the Lord Jesus whom they had come to know during His three years of ministry. Even on the day of His ascension, the Resurrected One, who disappeared in the cloud before His disciples' eyes, was the same Jesus whom they were familiar with.

It is easy to understand, then, the reaction of the exile on the island of Patmos when he suddenly heard behind him "a great voice, as of a trumpet" (1:10) and "as the sound of many waters" (1:15). When he turned around, he saw "one like unto the Son of man, clothed with a garment down to the foot, and girt about the paps with a golden girdle" (1:13). These were the insignia of both His priestly and His royal estate. As for His person, He was radiant, "as the sun shineth in his strength" (1:16). "His head and his hairs were white like wool, as white as snow; and his eyes were as a flame of fire; and his feet like unto fine brass. . . . Out of his mouth went a sharp twoedged sword" (1:14-16).

Upon seeing the Son of man, John fell down as though struck by lightning, like the prophet Daniel before him. "When I saw him," he wrote, "I fell at his feet as dead" (1:17). But for John, as for Daniel, the Lord had a life-giving gesture and a reassuring word. Placing His right hand on the overwhelmed disciple, He said to him: "Fear not; I am the first and the last: I am he that liveth, and was dead; and, behold, I am alive for evermore . . . and have the keys of hell and of death" (1:17, 18).

Through these comforting words the unknown person, presented simply as "one like unto the Son of man," revealed His identity. John recognized Him from His gentle gesture, from the sound of His voice, from the declaration of who He is, and from the reminder of His death and resurrection. Without any doubt it was the Lord Jesus, for whose testimony John was suffering exile and persecution while eagerly awaiting His return.

Had that glorious day arrived? John could easily have thought so, particularly since Jesus had declared concerning him: "If I will that he tarry till I come, what is that to thee?" Following which, says the evangelist, "then went this saying abroad among the brethren, that that disciple should not die" (John 21:22, 23). But without allowing John time to reflect on it, the Lord commanded him: "Write the things which thou hast seen, and the things which are, and the things which shall be hereafter" (1:19).

What had he seen? Very moving scenes connected with the history of God's people, a glimpse of the life of the church from its apostolic origins to the end of time, scenes of the great conflict between the powers of darkness and the Prince of light—pictures designed to give God's people of all centuries a clear understanding of the perils and conflicts the church would have to face. But before this, John beheld the Son of man working to ensure the triumph of God's cause both in heaven and on earth. His action covers the whole of our era, that is, from His resurrection to His triumphal second advent.

Although they cannot see Him, Christians should know that their Lord is walking among the golden lampstands, a symbol of His continual presence in the church. Jesus had promised His disciples: "And, lo, I am with you alway, even unto the end of the world" (Matthew 28:20). Moreover, in His right hand He holds the seven stars, which stand for "the angels of the seven churches" (1:20). This assures us that the Lord Himself is controlling the destiny of the church and that none of His faithful messengers can be snatched out of His hand.

At the beginning of the second vision, John saw "a door . . . opened in heaven," and he heard the voice of the Son of man saying to him: "Come up hither, and I will shew thee things which must be hereafter" (4:1). Then followed the majestic vision of the throne of God, and "in the midst of the throne . . . a Lamb as it had been slain" (5:6). This symbolic lamb, representing the crucified Christ, was not simply a reminder of the paschal lamb and the work of salvation. John observed the slain Lamb ministering in the heavenly sanctuary. He alone was worthy to open the seals (5:9). He saw Him make war on the enemies of God's people and overcome them (17:14). He observed Him carry out God's judgments (6:16, 17; 14:10) against all those whose name had not been "written in the book of life of the Lamb" (13:8; see 21:27). He saw Him before the throne of God with the redeemed who were singing "the song of the Lamb" (14:1, 2; 15:3) and on the mount of Zion, where the "marriage supper of the Lamb" takes place (19:7, 9). Finally he saw the Lamb Himself "feed" the redeemed and "lead them unto living fountains of waters" (7:17).

In the vision of the seven trumpets, which foretell the calamities that will strike Christianity during the course of the centuries, John witnessed the providential, exceptional intervention of the Son of man. Although He is not mentioned specifically, we can recognize Him easily in the person of the powerful messenger who descends from heaven "clothed with a cloud," His head crowned with a rainbow, His face shining "as it were the sun, and his feet as pillars of fire" (10:1). He intervenes at the end of time, before the last trumpet sounds and the mystery of God is accomplished. His object is to raise up a prophetic movement to proclaim God's last message to "many peoples, and nations, and tongues, and kings" (10:11).

Finally, the Son of man revealed Himself at the end of human history, at the culmination of the great conflict between the woman and the dragon, that is, between the church and the antichrist. "And I looked," wrote John, "and behold a white cloud, and upon the cloud one sat like unto the Son of man, having on his head a golden crown, and in his hand a sharp sickle: . . . for the time is come for thee to reap; for the harvest of the earth is ripe" (14:14, 15).

In His prophetic discourse Jesus had clearly described the same scene: "And then shall appear the sign of the Son of man in heaven: and then shall all the tribes of the earth mourn, and they shall see the Son of man coming in the clouds of heaven with power and great glory" (Matthew 24:30).

He also foretold the same scene to His judges as proof that He was truly the Christ, the Son of God: "I say unto you," He declared solemnly, "Hereafter shall ye see the Son of man sitting on the right hand of power, and coming in the clouds of heaven" (Matthew 26:64).

John certainly had this picture in mind when he wrote at the beginning of Revelation: "Behold, he cometh with clouds; and every eye shall see him, and they also which pierced him" (1:7).

This vision of the Son of man returning on the clouds of heaven is found again in chapter 19, verses 11 to 16, but this time the accent is placed on the triumphal aspect. In the wide-opened heavens the prophet of Patmos saw "the King of kings, and Lord of lords" appear, seated on a white horse. His eyes shone like a flame of fire and on His head were many crowns. Out of His mouth went a sharp sword to smite the nations whom He will rule with a rod of iron. His vesture was dipped in blood. "And the armies which were in heaven followed him upon white horses, clothed in fine linen, white and clean."

Such are the visions through which Jesus Christ is revealed in the Book of Revelation. A Jesus Christ of glory, majesty, power, and triumph. However, although He appears each time in the glory of heaven, Jesus Christ is never presented to us as an object for speculation, as an abstract being, or even as a purely heavenly spirit. John saw Him as "one like unto the Son of man," who is clearly identified by the names attributed to Him and by those He employs to make Himself known.

In Biblical times the name of a person generally corresponded to his character. It therefore revealed the person in his entirety. To know someone's name meant to have access to the secret of his personality, to know who he was and what he was. Revelation demonstrates this fact more clearly than any other book in the Bible. Accordingly, each name for the Son of man reveals a certain aspect of His being, His nature, His character, and His attributes. We should pause, then, to consider this other revelation of Jesus Christ.

Each time John spoke of his Lord, he called Him by one of the names found in the Gospels and the epistles: Jesus Christ, Christ, or Jesus. John certainly did not choose the names at random. On the contrary, each name is used in close relationship to the events described and in accordance with the specific significance of each name. Whoever is aware of the importance of numbers in Revelation will perhaps also discern a meaning in the frequency with which these names occur.

Thus, the name *Jesus Christ* appears three times in the introduction and the preface of the book (1:1, 2, 5). It is the name that Paul used in his epistles to make Jesus known to the Greek-Roman world. The name forms an indissoluble union between the historical person and the Anointed of God, the object of our faith. It recalls, too, the divine-human nature of Christ Jesus.

The name *Christ* is found seven times in the Greek of Revelation: three times in association with the name of Jesus as mentioned in the above paragraph, and four times in close connection with the name of God (11:15; 12:10; 20:4, 6). Furthermore, in these four passages the name appears in the context of the kingdom of God. Also John did not say "the Christ" or "Christ" as Paul or the evangelists did, but "the Christ of his [God's]" (greek) or "God, . . . and his Christ." By this he intended to underline the fact that God's Christ is truly the Anointed of God to whom God has given "the kingdoms of this world" so that He may reign with the redeemed "for ever and ever."

However, John seems to have prefered the name *Jesus*, meaning "Yahweh is salvation." He used it fourteen times with meaningful insistence when referring to the "testimony ["witness"] of Jesus" (1:9; 12:17; 19:10; 20:4), "the faith of Jesus" (14:12), the "martyrs of Jesus" (17:6), the "Lord Jesus" (22:20, 21), "Jesus Christ" (1:1, 2, 5), or just "Jesus" (22:16). For John this name evoked, without any doubt, the Beloved Person whom he had seen, heard, and touched, as he took pleasure in emphasizing at the beginning of his first epistle (1 John 1:1-3).

Only twice did John refer to the Son of man (1:13; 14:14), and even here he did so in a very impersonal way. Actually he allowed the Son of man to reveal Himself through the names He ascribed to Himself. In the first three chapters alone He introduces Himself approximately forty times either by one name or another, or by the expression translated "he that," "he which," or "who" followed by one of the attributes mentioned in the opening vision.

First of all, we have those names through which the Son of man revealed His divinity, that which He holds in common with God Himself. On three occasions He introduced Himself directly with the words "I am Alpha and Omega" (1:8; 21:6; 22:13). He also expressed the same divine prerogatives in three different ways: "I am Alpha and Omega, the beginning and the end, the first and the last" (Revelation 22:13; see also 1:17). These are the Creator's specific attributes that the prophet Isaiah reserved for God alone (Isaiah 41:4; 44:6; 48:12).

Elsewhere He declared Himself to be "the beginning of the creation of God" (3:14), that is, the actual creative "principle" through which "all things were made" (John 1:3; compare Hebrews 1:2). "For," as the apostle Paul wrote, "by him were all things created, that are in heaven, and that are in earth, visible and invisible, . . . all things were created by him, and for him" (Colossians 1:16).

To the names designed to reveal the Creator, the Son of man immediately added those names that present Him as possessing life in Himself, as the One who is the source of life, as the Eternal One. "I am he that liveth, . . . and, behold, I am alive for evermore" (1:18). By these words His identity with God is not only suggested but affirmed, since God is also called "the living God" (7:2), him that "liveth for ever and ever" (4:9, 10; 10:6; 15:7).

The Son of man used other divine names to reveal Himself to His church. Just once in Revelation He introduced Himself as the Son of God (2:18). And twice He attributed to Himself characteristics that belong only to God: "for thou only art holy" (15:4); "he that is holy, he that is true" and "the Amen" (3:7; 3:14).

Jesus Christ is revealed to us through yet other expressions: "The Word of God" (19:13), "the prince of the kings of the earth" (1:5), and the "Lord of lords, and King of kings" (17:14; see 19:16)—titles that have more of a connection with His functions than with His nature. Twice He called Himself the "witness," modified by the adjectives *faithful* and *true* (1:5; 3:14), and once He is called "Faithful and True" (19:11).

Finally there is the figurative use of the word *Lamb*, under which name there are depicted the various aspects and functions of the Messianic Suffering Servant.

But one name is missing, the name carried by the One who will mount the white horse during the final triumph. "The King of kings, and Lord of lords" "had a name . . . that no man knew, but he himself" (19:12). This might be the name that Paul spoke of "which is above every name" and which God will give to the One whom He has "highly exalted" so "that at the name of Jesus every knee should bow, of things in heaven, and things in earth, and things under the earth; and that every tongue should confess that Jesus Christ is Lord, to the glory of God the Father" (Philippians 2:9-11).

Chapter 2

The Testimony of Jesus to His Church

If, on the one hand, the Apocalypse is truly a revelation of the person of Jesus Christ, it is also, on the other hand, a message that is fundamentally "the testimony of Jesus." A close study of John's writings (Revelation, the fourth Gospel, and the three epistles) is immediately impressive because of the importance given to the concept of testimony. Words such as *witness, testimony,* and *testify* recur frequently under his pen, making this one of the chief characteristics of the Johannine writings.

Revelation, however, is the only book in the New Testament in which Jesus is called the Witness. Moreover, it is the first title ascribed to Jesus in the book, and John applied it to Him only once. Right at the beginning, in fact, John wished "the seven churches which are in Asia," "grace . . . and peace . . . from Jesus Christ, who is the faithful witness" (1:4, 5). On one occasion, also, the Son of man used the title Himself: "These things saith the Amen, the faithful and true witness" (3:14).

The word *witness* was also given to Jesus' disciples. The Master Himself said to them, "Ye shall be witnesses unto me" (Acts 1:8). However, according to John, Jesus is the only One able to carry the title Witness without qualification. The disciples were always witnesses *of Jesus.* Speaking of Antipas, put to death at Pergamos, Jesus said: "My faithful witness" (2:13, NEB*). Similarly, of the two prophets commissioned to prophesy for 1260 days, He said,

---

From The New English Bible. Copyright, The Delegates of the Oxford University Press and The Syndics of the Cambridge University Press, 1961, 1970. Reprinted by permission.

17

"my two witnesses" (11:3). Finally, it is written of "Babylon the great, the mother of harlots and abominations of the earth" (17:5) that she is "drunk with the blood of God's people and with the blood of those who had borne their testimony to Jesus" (17:6, NEB).

Although there are two types of witnesses: the witnesses of Jesus and Jesus Himself, there is only one witness, or testimony, "the testimony of Jesus." This typical expression recurs seven times in Revelation. First of all, referring to himself, John declared that he "bore witness to the word of God and to the testimony of Jesus Christ" (1:2, RSV). He further explained that he was exiled on the isle of Patmos "on account of the word of God and the testimony of Jesus" (1:9, RSV).

Nevertheless, John was not alone in possessing "the testimony of Jesus." The angel who appeared to him insisted, "I am thy fellowservant, and of thy brethren that have the testimony of Jesus" (19:10). Again, the Christians of the remnant church are said to "keep the commandments of God and bear testimony to Jesus" (12:17, RSV). Finally, on two other occasions, John stated that the souls who were slain or beheaded were killed "for the witness of Jesus, and for the word of God" (20:4; 6:9).

It is clear from these texts that "the testimony of Jesus" is the distinctive mark of Jesus' true followers, carried by the prophet of Patmos as well as by his brethren in the Apostolic Church. And according to the prophetic word, the remnant church must be characterized by "the testimony of Jesus" as well as by obedience to God's commandments. Of the church members, as of the prophet, it is said that they "have the testimony of Jesus."

But what exactly does having the testimony of Jesus mean? According to the Greek, this expression could very well be translated "the testimony given by Jesus" or "the testimony which comes from Jesus." That is why He is presented as the first witness, the witness par excellence, the only one to give a testimony that is perfectly "faithful and true." He Himself declared to His judges: "To this end was I born, and for this cause came I into the world, that I should bear witness unto the truth" (John 18:37). The apostle Paul stated that "Christ Jesus . . . witnessed a good confession" before Pontius Pilate (1 Timothy 6:13). Therefore, His disciples must also witness in the steps of their Master, as "witnesses of Jesus," to the extent that they "have the testimony of Jesus."

Nevertheless, the fact of being a witness of Jesus and possessing His testimony does not mean that the prophetic word is revealed in the same way to every witness and that everyone's testimony is of the same value. In his prologue to the Book of Revelation John set out very clearly a form of hierarchy in what can be considered as the process of the revelation of the prophetic word (1:1-3).

First, the record states, Jesus Christ is the One to whom God gave the revelation "to shew unto his servants things which must shortly come to pass" (1:1). Then Jesus, being the first witness, "sent and signified it by his angel unto his servant John" (1:1). The latter in turn conveyed it to the church by means of the written testimony. Finally, as the prophetic message is received by the members of the church, they become Jesus' witnesses in the world. It is to them that John addresses the first of the seven beatitudes of Revelation: "Blessed is he that readeth, and they that hear the words of this prophecy, and keep those things which are written therein" (1:3).

The same hierarchical principle is set forth by Jesus at the conclusion to the Book of Revelation, at the close of the visions: "These sayings are faithful and true: and the Lord God of the holy prophets sent his angel to shew unto his servants the things which must shortly be done. Behold, I come quickly: blessed is he that keepeth the sayings of the prophecy of this book" (22:6, 7).

There is an important difference, therefore, between the testimony given by Jesus to His servant John and the testimony given by the prophet of Patmos "to the seven churches which are in Asia." John receives "the testimony of Jesus" directly from heaven through a supernatural revelation, whereas the church and its members receive the same testimony through the prophet's inspired pen: "Write the things which thou hast seen, and the things which are, and the things which shall be hereafter" (1:19).

There is yet another difference between the testimony rendered by the prophet and that given by the church. The prophet renders his testimony primarily for the benefit of the church (1 Corinthians 14:22). It was "unto the fathers" that God spoke in the past "by the prophets," "at sundry times and in divers manners," and it is "unto us" that He has spoken in these last days "by his Son" (Hebrews 1:1, 2). The church, on the other hand, is called to spread "the testimony of Jesus" in the world, where its members are to "shine as lights" "in the midst of a crooked and perverse nation," "holding forth the word of life" (Philippians 2:15, 16). Such is the command given by Jesus to His witnesses of all times: "Ye are the light of the world. . . . Let your light so shine before men, that they may see your good works, and glorify your Father which is in heaven" (Matthew 5:14-16).

The same distinctions must be made when "the testimony of Jesus" is considered as "the spirit of prophecy," in harmony with the angel's own definition (19:10). Without doubt this definition of the spirit of prophecy applies first and in a very special way to the testimony of the prophets to whom God supernaturally reveals "things which must shortly come to pass" (1:1). But the same Spirit who inspires the prophets to write down their testimony also sheds His influence on those who read, understand, and keep the prophetic words. Whoever has "the testimony of Jesus" must necessarily possess "the spirit of prophecy" to a greater or lesser degree, either as a prophet or as a disciple.

One of the characteristics of the Apostolic Church was that it had "the testimony of Jesus," that is, the "spirit of prophecy." This was manifested at first by the gift of prophecy within the church and then by the testimony given to the world by its members, many of whom did so at the cost of their lives. Ellen White confirmed this when she wrote: "When the fifth seal was opened, John the Revelator in vision saw beneath the altar the company that were slain for the Word of God and the testimony of Jesus Christ" (Manuscript 39, 1906, *The Seventh-day Adventist Bible Commentary*, Vol. 7, p. 968).

According to the revelations given to John, the believers who constitute "the remnant of her [the woman's] seed" are indicated as possessing the same characteristics. The remnant church is not only distinguished by its observation of "the commandments of God" but also by the "testimony of Jesus" (12:17), that is, the "spirit of prophecy" (19:10). We understand this to have two meanings. First, it refers to the gift of prophecy such as was exercised in the past by the prophets whom the Spirit of Christ moved to speak for God. Second, it describes the testimony based on the word of prophecy that the church and its members render.

It is generally thought that the gift of prophecy was only connected with the formation of the Scriptural canon and that it consequently ceased to manifest itself in the church after the death of the apostles. This is not what the New Testament teaches, however. The Bible mentions several true prophets, both men and women, whose spoken or written messages are not to be found in the Sacred Canon. The apostle Paul not only affirmed the necessity of the gift of prophecy in the church's edification but also gave it pride of place among all the other spiritual gifts (Romans 12:6-8; Ephesians 4:11-13). He exhorted the Christians in Thessalonica not to despise the prophets (1 Thessalonians 5:20), and to the Christians at Corinth, proud in their possession of certain spiritual gifts, he recommended the gift of prophecy above all others: "Desire spiritual gifts, but rather that ye may prophesy" (1 Corinthians 14:1). For, he declares, "He that prophesieth speaketh unto men to edification, and exhortation, and comfort. . . . He that prophesieth edifieth the church" (1 Corinthians 14:3, 4).

In His prophetic sermon Jesus several times warned the disciples against being led astray by false prophets (Matthew 24:4, 5, 11, 24). Their deceptions will be particularly subtle just before the Second Coming, "insomuch that, if it were possible, they shall deceive the very elect" (verse 24). His warning against the false manifestations of the gift of prophecy leads one to assume that there must exist at the same time an authentic manifestation of this gift. Otherwise it would have been sufficient for Jesus to have warned the church against all the prophets who would come after

Him and His disciples. Such is not the case, however. As Ellen G. White explicitly states, "The very last deception of Satan will be to make of none effect the testimony of the Spirit of God" (*Selected Messages*, Book One, p. 48) as it must be revealed in the remnant church during the last days.

The role of the prophet and Christ's disciples is not only to testify to Jesus but also to the Word of God. This is clearly apparent from the texts referring to the testimony of Jesus. The prophet of Patmos stressed the fact that he "bare record of the word of God, and of the testimony of Jesus Christ." Four times the testimony of Jesus is associated in this way with the Word of God (1:2, 9; 6:9; 20:4; compare also 12:17), as though they were one and the same. It is a fact that the Word of God testifies to Jesus (John 5:39) and that the testimony of Jesus can only be made in reference to the Word of God. In this John simply echoed Isaiah's prophecy: "To the law and to the testimony" (Isaiah 8:20).

We must consider the testimonies of Ellen G. White in the same way: "The written testimonies are not to give new light, but to impress vividly upon the heart the truths of inspiration already revealed. . . . The *Testimonies* are not to belittle the word of God, but to exalt it and attract minds to it" (Ellen G. White, *Testimonies for the Church*, Vol. 5, p. 665).

In the Revelation John sets us the example. No other New Testament book gives greater testimony to Jesus Christ through constant reference to the Word of God. Words, expressions, and quotations from the Old Testament are woven throughout the book. John knew that "the testimony of Jesus," as revealed to him, was truly the fulfillment of that which the prophets before him had written. That is why, in describing his visions, he continually referred to words, expressions, and themes drawn from Sacred Writ. For him, as for Jesus, the revelation that he received and of which he must testify was the accomplishment of "all things . . . which were written in the law of Moses, and in the prophets, and in the psalms" (Luke 24:44).

One last aspect merits our attention with regard to the

testimony to be given to Jesus. It arises from the use of *to testify*. On the four occasions that the verb appears in Revelation (1:2; 22:16, 18, 20), the act of testifying applies directly to the book itself. On the one hand, because it contains Jesus' own testimony: "I Jesus have sent mine angel to testify unto you these things in the churches" (22:16) and He "which testifieth these things saith, Surely I come quickly" (22:20).

On the other hand, because it is a testimony given by John, who wrote the book as he was commanded to do so by Jesus: "John, who bore witness to the word of God and to the testimony of Jesus Christ, even to all that he saw" (1:2, RSV). Moreover, at the end of his mission John declared solemnly: "I testify unto every man that heareth the words of the prophecy of this book, If any man shall add unto these things, God shall add unto him the plagues that are written in this book" (22:18).

Through these statements Jesus and John declare the authenticity of their testimony. They both desire to guarantee that their "sayings are faithful and true" (22:6) in such a way that if anyone adds or takes "away from the words of the book of this prophecy, God shall take away his part out of the book of life, and out of the holy city" (22:19). But the ones who read and those who "hear the words of this prophecy, and keep those things which are written therein" (1:3) are declared to be happy or blessed both by John in the introduction and by Jesus in the final message (22:7). For them the promises of God will be fulfilled. They "shall inherit all things" (21:7) and will "have right to the tree of life, and may enter in through the gates into the city" (22:14).

As has been said, "We can only properly comprehend the Book of Revelation if we realize that it presents Christians with the testimony they must give to the world. The visions show us the witnesses of Jesus announcing the contents of the book. The usefulness of St. John's book is that it provides Christians with the formula as well as the meaning of their testimony" (J. Combin, *Le Christ dans l'Apocalypse*, p. 133).

"We have been given a message exceeding in importance any other message ever entrusted to mortals. This message Christ came in person to the Isle of Patmos to present to John. He told him to write down what he saw and heard during his vision, that the churches might know what was to come upon the earth. . . . It is time for a great change to take place among the people who are looking for the second appearing of their Lord. Soon strange things will take place. God will hold us responsible for the way in which we treat the truth" (Ellen G. White, *The Medical Ministry*, pp. 37, 38).

The importance of studying the Book of Revelation for the spiritual life of the church in general and for each individual Christian in particular can never be overemphasized. That is why "there should be a closer and more diligent study of the Revelation, and a more earnest presentation of the truths it contains—truths which concern all who are living in these last days" (Ellen G. White, *Evangelism*, p. 197). "If our people were half awake, if they realized the nearness of the events portrayed in the Revelation, a reformation would be wrought in our churches, and many more would believe the message" (Ellen G. White, *Testimonies to Ministers*, p. 118).

When Jesus Christ appeared to John at Patmos, He did not do so merely to encourage His beloved disciple who was confined in lonely exile. He appeared to John primarily to entrust him with a message for the church.

"I John, your brother, who share with you in Jesus the tribulation and the kingdom and the patient endurance, was on the island called Patmos on account of the word of God and the testimony of Jesus. I was in the Spirit on the Lord's day, and I heard behind me a loud voice like a trumpet saying, 'Write what you see in a book and send it to the seven churches, to Ephesus and to Smyrna and to Pergamum and to Thyatira and to Sardis and to Philadelphia and to Laodicea' " (1:9-11, RSV).

Then after making Himself known to John, the Son of man repeated the command: "Write the things which thou hast seen, and the things which are, and the things which shall be hereafter" (1:19). The same instruction is renewed before each of the seven letters dictated to the prophet:

"Unto the angel of the church of Ephesus write," "Unto the angel of the church in Smyrna write," and so on.

These seven churches in the province of Asia really existed, as did the cities whose names they carry. Archaeological discoveries of the past few years have brought forth to us historical proof of their existence. From the accounts related in *The Acts of the Apostles* by Ellen G. White we know that several of these churches owed their origin to the ministry of Paul and his fellow laborers. Some of their names are also found in the epistles written by the great apostle.

Moreover, it is certain that the seven churches mentioned here were not the only churches in Asia, nor even the most important ones. The choice of seven, the meaning of their names, as well as their geographical location evidently carry a symbolic significance.

The seven cities that contained these Christian communities were all connected by the imperial road in the Roman province of Asia. The road made a complete circle—going northward from Ephesus, the capital, to Pergamum [Pergamos, KJV] by way of Smyrna; turning eastward then southward it passed through Thyatira, Sardis, Philadelphia, and Laodicea, and finally it linked up again with Ephesus.

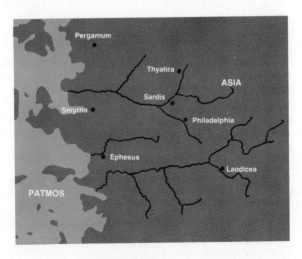

However, the selection of these particular churches was undoubtedly influenced by the etymological meaning of their names, which clearly have a symbolic significance. This meaning alone sums up the general character of the period of church history that each church represents.

Finally, the figure seven leaves no doubt whatsoever as to the symbolic meaning of the messages contained in these letters. Seven is a sacred number to the Bible writers, especially to the author of the Book of Revelation, who uses this number and its adjective form fifty-nine times. The number seven signifies "fullness," "universality," and "perfection."

So it is that many interpreters of Revelation over the centuries have considered the seven churches as symbols of seven great periods in the history of Christ's church from its beginning to the end of time. Confirming this interpretation, Ellen G. White wrote: "The names of the seven churches are symbolic of the church in different periods of the Christian Era. The number 7 indicates completeness, and is symbolic of the fact that the messages extend to the end of time, while the symbols used reveal the condition of the church at different periods in the history of the world" (*The Acts of the Apostles,* p. 585).

This interpretation can also be suggested by the vision of the Son of man walking "in the midst of the seven candlesticks" (1:13), which are "the seven churches" (1:20). This not only can represent Christ's continual presence among His people "even unto the end of the world" (Matthew 28:20), but it can also indicate a progression through time, a movement through space, namely, a certain historical development.

Therefore the picture of Christ walking among the seven lampstands, moving from one church to another, can constitute a summary of the history of Christ's church from the first century to our day, with a prophetic message addressed to each.

This does not mean, however, that the message must be limited to the literal or symbolic church to which it was addressed. Paul's epistles, written to specific churches, have a message for us today just as much as they did for the

Christians to whom they were originally intended.

The spiritual problems of the seven churches are typical ones. Therefore, each time the same conditions recur, the Lord's exhortations, reproaches, threats, counsels, and promises retain their full value. This can also be seen from the conclusion to each message: "He that hath an ear, let him hear what the Spirit saith unto the churches" (2:7, 11, 17, 29; 3:6, 13, 22).

These messages clearly contain a universal application. As such, they concern us all, collectively and individually, as disciples of Christ. Ellen G. White does not suggest otherwise when she applies the messages addressed to the churches of Ephesus and Sardis to the present-day church (*Testimonies for the Church,* Vol. 8, pp. 98, 99; *Review and Herald,* February 25, 1902).

A quick glance at the seven letters and a brief comparison between them makes one immediately aware of the similarity in their style. The layout of the letters follows a unique pattern. The different parts of each letter are always introduced by certain stereotyped phrases.

Naturally, we find the address at the beginning of each letter. The addressee is always the leader of the church in one of the seven towns, the name of which follows. The opening phrase is invariably the same: "Unto the angel of the church of . . . write."

The Greek word *angelos* literally means "messenger" or "the one who is sent." The Bible uses it of a human envoy as well as of a heavenly messenger (Matthew 11:10; Luke 7:24; 9:52; James 2:25). Paul reminded the Galatians that they had received him "as an angel of God" (4:14).

The angels to whom the seven letters are addressed represent, therefore, the leaders of each church community—the elders and the pastors—who have the responsibility of passing the message on to the church. They are represented by the seven stars that the Son of man holds in His right hand (1:20).

"These words are spoken to the teachers in the church—those entrusted by God with weighty responsibilities. The sweet influences that are to be abundant in the church are bound up with God's ministers, who are to reveal the love of Christ. The stars of heaven are under His control. He fills them with light. He guides and directs their movements. If He did not do this, they would become fallen stars. So with His ministers. They are but instruments in His hands, and all the good they accomplish is done through His power. Through them His light is to shine forth" (*The Acts of the Apostles*, pp. 586, 587).

After the address and according to the custom of the time, we find the name of the sender. True, He is never named directly but is introduced by a phrase such as: "These things saith he. . . ." Jesus then reveals Himself by one of the attributes of the Son of man, described by John in the opening vision. These are always directly related to the content of the message. Moreover, Christ appears each time in His double mediatorial role, both as God's representative to men and man's representative before God.

The body of the letter inself contains a brief description of the spiritual condition of the church community. Like a perfect teacher, Jesus usually begins with a few words of praise, invariably introduced by the phrase: "I know. . . ." For indeed, only He knows the exact condition of each church. He is, therefore, also unique in assessing the merits and judging the weaknesses of each one. Hence the reproaches are often followed by threats. But in every case the Lord has a word of exhortation, counsel, and encouragement.

On three occasions the reproaches are introduced by the phrase "Nevertheless I have somewhat against thee" (2:4, 14, 20) or in similar language. The exhortation is not preceded by any particular phrase, but the Master's advice is always given in the imperative form: "Repent," "Be . . . faithful," "Be zealous."

Finally, the conclusion of each letter always includes two aspects. First, a warning or a call to be especially watchful, such as Jesus often used during His earthly ministry at the conclusion of several of His sermons: "He that hath an ear, let him hear what the Spirit saith unto the churches." Second, there is a definitely eschatological promise—one that will be fulfilled at the end of time, when all things shall be made new. This is furthermore expressed through a symbol whose exact meaning can only be understood when compared with the final vision of the heavenly city in chapters 21 and 22. Concerning the conclusion to each letter, it is important to notice that the warning is always addressed to the individual believers in all churches, whereas the promise is only made to the one who "overcometh."

Other interesting details also merit our attention. In comparing the contents of each of the letters, the first thing we notice is that the Laodicean church is the only one that does not receive praise. On the other hand, the churches of Smyrna and Philadelphia are given special praise and are not reproached in any way.

We also see that the odd-numbered letters (first, third, fifth, and seventh) are addressed to the churches where evil predominates over good. They are the most severely judged. In complete contrast, the even-numbered letters (second, fourth, and sixth) are addressed to the churches where good triumphs over evil.

Finally, let us make a last observation regarding chronology. Since the letters to the seven churches do not form a time prophecy, no absolute dates can be set. The beginning or the end of a particular period is, therefore, difficult to fix. However, the details contained in the various messages allow us to identify the different periods of the Christian church without great difficulty.

THE LETTERS TO THE 7 CHURCHES

CHURCH	EPHESUS	SMYRNA	PERGAMUM
PERIOD	1st cent	2nd–3rd cent	4th–6th cent
SIGNIFICANCE	DESIRABLE The apostolic church	BITTERNESS The persecuted church	CITADEL-ELEVATION The popular church
CHRIST'S INTRODUCTION	He that holds 7 stars and walks in midst of candlesticks	The First and the Last, He who was dead and is alive	He that hath the sharp two-edged sword
COMMENDATION	Patience, good works, and tested false teachers	Perseverance in tribulation Rich in spiritual things	Held fast My name and have not denied My faith
REPROOF	Left thy first love	None	False teachings
EXHORTATION	Repent and do the first works.	Do not fear. Be faithful.	Repent.
PROMISE	The tree of life	The crown of life	Hidden manna, white stone, a new name

THYATIRA	SARDIS	PHILADELPHIA	LAODICEA
6th–16th cent	16th–18th cent	18th–19th cent	19th–20th cent
SACRIFICE OF VICTIMS The compromising church	REMNANT The reformed church	BROTHERLY LOVE The awakening church	JUDGING OF THE PEOPLE The church of the time of judgment
The Son of God, whose eyes are like a flame of fire and feet like brass	He that hath the 7 Spirits and the 7 stars	He that is holy, true, and hath the key of David	The Faithful and True Witness
Love, service, faith, and patience	Faithfulness of some	Loyalty and patience	None
False teachings; Jezebel harbored	You are dead.	None	Lukewarmness and pretension
Repent and hold fast to that thou hast.	Repent. Be vigilant.	Hold that fast which thou hast.	Buy gold, white raiment, eyesalve, and repent.
Power over the nations and the morning star	White robes, names written in the book of life	Pillar in the temple of God	With Christ on His throne

Chapter 3

The Messages of Jesus to the Churches of the Early Centuries

The first two letters dictated to John by Jesus are addressed to the churches at Ephesus and Smyrna, representing the Apostolic Church of the first century and the church of the imperial persecutions respectively. The messages given to them are not merely of historical interest, but their chief concern is the spiritual life of the churches in this period. Therefore, they are of equal interest to us.

Letter to the Church of Ephesus

There are several possible reasons why Ephesus can symbolize the Apostolic Church and illustrate the spiritual life of the first-generation Christians.

It was the most important town in the Roman province of Asia. It was, in fact, its political and religious capital. The proconsuls resided in Ephesus. The goddess Artemis, the Diana of the Ephesians, had an imposing temple there. Another temple, dedicated to Roma and Augustus, became the center of imperial worship under Emperor Domitian—the one who probably exiled John.

From the Christian point of view Ephesus was also a very important center. The first church in the province of Asia was founded there, around the year AD 52, during Paul's second missionary journey (Acts 18:24 to 19:41). For two years Paul and his fellow laborers preached throughout the country, "so that all they which dwelt in Asia heard the word of the Lord Jesus" (Acts 19:10).

According to tradition, John settled in Ephesus after the destruction of Jerusalem in AD 70. Up until his death at the beginning of the second century he is thought to have exercised a fruitful ministry there. It is also from Ephesus that he is thought to have been exiled to Patmos, probably between AD 96 and 98. During the centuries that followed, Ephesus was the seat of a number of councils, and it was even the capital of the Eastern Christian church before Constantinople.

Ephesus may have been chosen to represent the first period in the history of the Christian church due to the suggested meaning of its name—the Desirable One. The Christian church of the first century remains unquestionably the ideal model, although it was not without defects.

In His message to the church of Ephesus, Jesus introduces Himself through the symbol of Him "who walketh in the midst of the seven golden candlesticks" (2:1). By this reference the Lord assured the early church of His care, His presence, and His help.

The praise given to the church of Ephesus relates to its works, its labor, and its perseverance. Amid a hostile world it gave an unsurpassed and beautiful example of fraternity and fellowship: "And the multitude of them that believed were of one heart and of one soul: neither said any of them that ought of the things which he possessed was his own; but they had all things common" (Acts 4:32).

By its conquering power the Apostolic Church spread the knowledge of the gospel among all the nations of the time, despite many and varied difficulties. Moreover, through its vigilance, it preserved the purity of faith and morals, for it did not tolerate evil ones and false brethren any more than it did false shepherds and false apostles (2:2). Its attitude toward the Nicolaitans, members of a heretical sect whose works displeased the Lord, is especially mentioned (2:6). Finally, its endurance in trial was not forgotten by the One for whose name the church was suffering unwearyingly (2:3).

Unfortunately, as the years went by the church of Ephesus gradually lost that which had made it so desirable. "Nevertheless I have somewhat against thee, because thou hast left thy first love" (2:4). When love disappears, nothing—absolutely nothing—can replace it. The apostle Paul expressed this beautifully in 1 Corinthians 13:1-3: "Though I . . . and have not charity, I am nothing. And though I bestow all my goods to feed the poor, and though I give my body to be burned, and have not charity, it profiteth me nothing."

Love distinguishes the true Christian. "By this shall all men know that ye are my disciples, if ye have love one to another" (John 13:35). No longer is it a matter of simply "Thou shalt love thy neighbour as thyself." According to His new commandment, Jesus said, "We should 'love one another, as I have loved you' " (John 15:12). In the upper chamber Jesus prayed that His own would manifest this love so that the world might believe in the One whom God had sent into the world to save the world (John 3:17; 17:21). "Bond of perfectness" (Colossians 3:14), this love alone can lead to unity "of . . . heart and . . . soul" (Acts 4:32), such as existed in the Apostolic Church.

There is only one remedy for spiritual decline, one alone, that proposed by Jesus. It involves three successive steps and is a brief summary of the three phases of all true conversion: awakening of conscience, repentance, and the practice of good works inspired by love.

"Remember therefore from whence thou are fallen" (2:5) is the first part of Jesus' practical counsel. In other words, "Recognize that you no longer possess your first love." This awakening is essential. No improvement can be hoped for as long as this does not take place. Thus the value of repentance, the second step set forth by Jesus directly depends on an awakened conscience.

"Repent" is the second part of the Master's advice. This call will be sounded forth to all the churches where the Lord is obliged to make reproaches. Repentance primarily involves a change in one's way of thinking, as the Greek verb *metanoeō* implies.

If repentance is sincere, it will be evidenced subsequently by the actions. And this is the third part to Jesus' counsel: "Do the first works." Jesus calls for the church to carry out its first works, that is, works of love. When love is present, it must express itself through action. Similarly, faith and works are inseparable. And if it is clear that not one can be saved by his works, it is equally clear that everyone will be judged according to the good or the evil he has done. God "will render to every man according to his deeds: to them who by patient continuance in well doing seek for glory and honour and immortality, eternal life: but unto them that are contentious, and do not obey the truth, but obey unrighteousness, indignation and wrath" (Romans 2:6-8). Jesus also affirms this at the end of Revelation: "And, behold, I come quickly; and my reward is with me, to give every man according as his work shall be" (22:12).

In actual fact the Lord does not wait until His return before taking action: "I will come unto thee quickly, and will remove thy candlestick out of his place, except thou repent" (2:5). The threat leaves no doubt whatsoever. Should the flame of first love fail to burn anew, the Lord will remove the lampstand from its place.

God's warnings are never without consequence for those who ignore them, and those who listen to what the Spirit says can be sure of the Lord's promises. The promise given to the Ephesians is for all those who personally follow Jesus' counsel by either keeping alive or rekindling the flame of their first love. "To him that overcometh will I give to eat of the tree of life, which is in the midst of the paradise of God" (2:7).

Among the signs of the times, Jesus foretold a general decline in love: "And because iniquity shall abound, the love of many shall wax cold" (Matthew 24:12). Similarly, when speaking to the Laodicean church, Jesus says that it is neither hot nor cold but lukewarm (3:15). And so the remedy proposed to the church of Ephesus also concerns us.

"I am instructed to say that these words [Revelation 2:4, 5] are applicable to Seventh-day Adventist churches in their present condition. The love of God has been lost, and this means the absence of love for one another. Self, self, self, is cherished, and is striving for the supremacy. How long is this to continue? Unless there is a reconversion, there will soon be such a lack of godliness that the Church will be represented by the barren fig tree. . . . God help His people to make an application of this lesson while there is still time" (Ellen G. White, *Review and Herald*, February 25, 1902).

"He that hath an ear, let him hear what the Spirit saith

unto the churches" (2:7).

Letter to the Church of Smyrna

Through the prophet Isaiah, the Lord made the following well-known declaration concerning His Word: "It shall not return unto me void, but it shall accomplish that which I please, and it shall prosper in the thing whereto I sent it" (55:11).

Because the church of Ephesus did not listen to Jesus' counsel, He had to take away its lampstand. What in the beginning had only been a conditional threat finally became a sad reality, because the word of the Lord is never spoken without effect.

History teaches that a profound change took place within Christendom following the death of the apostles and the destruction of Jerusalem. The first generation of Christians, mainly converts from Judaism, was succeeded by another generation of believers who were mainly drawn from the Greek-Roman world. And so the church at Smyrna can represent the second period in the history of Christianity, that of the imperial persecutions. The year AD 95 marks the beginning of the persecutions related to emperor worship under Domitian, and persecution ended in AD 313 with the Edict of Milan. By signing this edict Emperor Constantine gave the Christian church the right to exist alongside the other religions. Furthermore, by his conversion to Christianity in AD 323 Christianity became the official religion of the empire. Thus the church of Smyrna clearly marks the transition between Ephesus (the Apostolic Church) and Pergamum (the triumphant church which was courted by the imperial power).

Indeed, the word *Smyrna* may express exactly what these two centuries of suffering and persecution represented for the church. Some interpreters have suggested that the name owes its origin to myrrh and signifies both "bitter" and an "agreeable odor." Myrrh is a bitter aromatic substance with a pleasing scent and was formerly used to embalm the dead. No other name, therefore, could better symbolize the bitter experience of a church that experienced persecutions, the catacombs, and martyrdom. For following the example of Jesus, whose sacrifice was "a sweetsmelling savour" (Ephesians 5:2), the church of Smyrna was able to add the "sweet savour of Christ" (2 Corinthians 2:15) to the bitterness of myrrh.

Like the church at Ephesus, the Christian community at Smyrna probably owed its origin to Paul's missionary work. Its name, however, is only found mentioned in Revelation. The town itself was renowned for the beauty of its location, and the ancients called it "the ornament of Asia." Situated on the edge of the Aegean Sea thirty-five miles north of Ephesus, it was also the birthplace of the famous Greek writer Homer. Smyrna has survived the changing fortunes of history, and it exists today under the Turkish name of Izmir. Nevertheless, few towns through the centuries have experienced more sieges, massacres, earthquakes, fires, and plagues than has Smyrna.

Like the town whose name it bears, the church of Smyrna endured more suffering than the other churches. Therefore, the titles under which Jesus introduces Himself here assume a significance that corresponds exactly to the situation: "These things saith the first and the last, which was dead, and is alive" (2:8). Through these words, the Lord assures the church that He is the Almighty and the Living One, in spite of external appearances. To those who are suffering because of His name and to the martyrs of the faith, Jesus reveals Himself as the One who has likewise suffered, who died, but who came back to life.

Jesus does not ignore the tragic circumstances surrounding the church of Smyrna: "I know thy works, and tribulation, and poverty, (but thou art rich)" (2:9). Extreme physical poverty, yes; but such spiritual riches that the world was enriched through them. The same contrast is found in the letter to the church at Laodicea (3:17). However, it is the reverse here.

To the persecutions inflicted on her by the pagan world were added "the blasphemy of them which say they are Jews, and are not, but are the synagogue of Satan" (2:9). During the second century, Jewish accusations against Christians reached their climax. Among other things, they charged Christians with falsifying the Scriptures—the very people who did not hesitate to suffer and die "for the word of God, and for the testimony of Jesus." The Book of Acts portrays the Jews as originating most of the persecutions against the church. The Jews at Smyrna in AD 155 cheered for Polycarp's martyrdom at the stake when he refused to swear by the fortune of Caesar and to say of the Christians, "away with the atheists."

From these dramatic circumstances it is not difficult to understand why Jesus' exhortation contains no reproach or threats. However, He does not conceal the suffering that still awaits the faithful in the church of Smyrna: "Fear none of those things which thou shalt suffer: behold, the devil shall cast some of you into prison, that ye may be tried; and ye shall have tribulation ten days" (2:10).

After two centuries of intermittent persecution, the devil reached the ultimate of his machinations against the church of Smyrna in the "tribulation [of] ten days"—or ten literal years according to the Biblical principle that a day equals one year (Numbers 14:34; Ezekiel 4:6). This tribulation was carried under Emperor Diocletian, who thought he could exterminate forever the Christian church, which to his mind threatened both the spirit and the life of imperial society. Beginning in AD 303, the tribulation announced by the prophecy lasted ten years until Constantine ended the persecution by signing the Edict of Milan in AD 313.

Because she was "faithful unto death," in accordance with the command given here, the church of Smyrna received the promise of the "crown of life" (2:10). Moreover, to all who overcome, the Lord also promises that they "shall not be hurt of the second death" (2:11), which is the destruction of the wicked "in the lake which burneth with fire and brimstone" (see 21:8; 20:6).

By her faithfulness the church of Smyrna ensured the triumph of Christianity in the Roman Empire. A new period in the history of the church of Christ was about to begin, represented first by the church of Pergamum and then by that of Thyatira.

Chapter 4

The Messages of Jesus to the Churches of the Middle Ages

What the adversary could not achieve by persecution, trials, and suffering, he would try now to obtain under the cloak of the church's triumph, by the dangerous allurement of prosperity and temporal honor. In his letter to the Thessalonians the apostle Paul had foretold the subtle and imperceptible penetration into the heart of the church of what he calls "the mystery of iniquity." Furthermore, he specified in 2 Thessalonians 2:3-7 that before the Lord returns there would "come a falling away first."

"But as persecution ceased, and Christianity entered the courts and palaces of kings, she laid aside the humble simplicity of Christ and His apostles for the pomp and pride of pagan priests and rulers; and in place of the requirements of God, she substituted human theories and traditions. The nominal conversion of Constantine, in the early part of the fourth century, caused great rejoicing; and the world, cloaked with a form of righteousness, walked into the church. Now the work of corruption rapidly progressed. Paganism, while appearing to be vanquished, became the conqueror. Her spirit controlled the church. Her doctrines, ceremonies, and superstitions were incorporated into the faith and worship of the professed followers of Christ" (Ellen G. White, *The Great Controversy*, pp. 49, 50).

The history of these tragic changes in the Christian church is depicted exactly in the two letters addressed to the churches at Pergamum and Thyatira. The first letter concerns the church that the imperial power wooed from AD 313 to 538; the second, the Western Empire church that dominated the world from AD 538 to 1798.

Letter to the Church of Pergamum

What we know of the church at Pergamum, we know only from the letter given in the Revelation. It owes its choice to the possible meaning of its name and to the fact that the city and church constitute a perfect symbol of the Christian church in the fourth and fifth centuries.

The etymology of the name *Pergamum* remains uncertain. The meaning often given is derived from the topographical situation of the city, which was built on an eminence, and so it dominated the plain like a strong castle. Hence its meaning of "citadel," "acropolis," or "elevation."

Built as it was on a rock, with natural defenses, the city seemed impregnable. It was never captured except by stratagem. Lysimachus, one of the four successors to Alexander the Great, made it his capital because he regarded it as the safest city of his kingdom.

Pergamum was famous for its altar to Zeus, which has been reconstructed and is now in the Pergamon Museum in East Berlin. It was the site of many heathen cults, and it is worthy of notice that the kings of Pergamum also led out in these religions as priest-kings. It was also at Pergamum that for the first time a Roman emperor was worshiped as a god—in 29 BC. A temple was then built there to the goddess Roma and to the emperor Augustus. These many significant details facilitate the interpretation of the contents of the letter to the church at Pergamum and the historical period represented by this church.

The symbol by which Jesus reveals Himself directly relates to the particular circumstances in the church of Pergamum. "These things saith he which hath the sharp sword with two edges" (2:12). Here is a reference to the "sharp twoedged sword" that John saw coming out of the mouth of the Son of man (1:16; see 19:15)—a symbol of the Word of God, "the sword of the Spirit" (Ephesians 6:17). The Lord intends to judge the spiritual situation of the church of Pergamum by the Word. "For the word of God is quick, and powerful, and sharper than any twoedged sword, piercing even to the dividing asunder of soul and spirit, and of the joints and marrow, and is a discerner of the thoughts and intents of the heart. Neither is there any creature that is not manifest in his sight: but all things are naked and opened unto the eyes of him with whom we have to do" (Hebrews 4:12, 13).

The situation in the church of Pergamum was such that only faithfulness to God's Word could keep it from falling into Satan's snares. As the Lord indicates: "I know . . . where thou dwellest, even where Satan's seat is" (2:13). Certainly it was praiseworthy for the church of Pergamum to have been able to establish itself in an unfavorable environment, a veritable stronghold of paganism—where the adversary had his "seat," that is, where he exercised his power in a very special way.

It is interesting to note that among other heathen cults, Pergamum had the monopoly on the worship of Aesculapius, the god of miraculous healing, whose emblem was the serpent. It appeared on many coins of the period, and even today the serpent symbolizes the medical fraternity. As is well known, the figure also represents Satan in the Bible. Elsewhere in the Revelation he is named "the great dragon, . . . that old serpent, called the Devil, and Satan, which deceiveth the whole world" (12:9).

Jesus commends still another trait in the church of Pergamum: "Thou holdest fast my name, and hast not denied my faith, even in those days . . . [of] Antipas" (2:13). On this last point we know nothing definite. It probably concerns a Christian who was martyred at Pergamum for refusing to worship the emperor. He "was slain among you, where Satan dwelleth" (2:13)—in the very temple of the adversary.

This literal interpretation in no way invalidates a symbolic interpretation. During the period represented by the church of Pergamum, there were several "Antipases" in the church, that is to say Antipaters. "Anti" can mean against, "pater" can mean father or pope. Certain commentators wish to see in this word a collective name for the group of fourth- and fifth-century believers who opposed the development of the hierarchy and in particular the power of the bishop in Rome. The latter ill-treated them, and a large number were put to death among them, in the Christian church, "where Satan dwelleth."

Having failed to conquer Christ's church through the violence of persecution, the adversary took it by stratagem from inside as he laid the foundation of a politico-religious system. "Under a cloak of pretended Christianity, Satan was insinuating himself into the church, to corrupt their faith and turn their minds from the word of truth. . . . It required a desperate struggle for those who would be faithful to stand firm against the deceptions and abominations which were disguised in sacerdotal garments and introduced into the church" (*The Great Controversy*, pp. 43-45).

By recalling the story of Balaam (Numbers 22–25; 31:13-16), Christ's reproach to the church of Pergamum emphasizes precisely the insidious action of the adversary. Balaam, the prophet of Satan, had advised King Balak to seduce the people of God. What he could not do by threats, he succeeded in doing through seduction by putting "a stumblingblock before the children of Israel, to eat things sacrificed unto idols, and to commit fornication" (2:14).

The Lord continues, "So hast thou also them that hold the doctrine of the Nicolaitanes" (2:15). We do not know exactly what they taught, but the Lord praised the Apostolic Church because it hated "the deeds of the Nicolaitanes" (2:6). The fact then that the church of Pergamum had accepted this doctrine shows an obvious sign of apostasy.

Once again the Lord makes an appeal to repent, followed by a warning: "Repent; or else I will come unto thee quickly, and will fight against them with the sword of my mouth" (2:16). In other words, the Lord will not remain indifferent to the situation in His church. If no repentance takes place, He will not hesitate to execute judgment on the apostates by means of His Word, "the sword of the Spirit."

But "to him that overcometh will I give to eat of the hidden manna, and will give him a white stone, and in the stone a new name written, which no man knoweth saving he that receiveth it" (2:17). The Spirit promises three things: "the hidden manna," that is to say the bread of life which is in Christ (John 6:31-33); "a white stone," a symbol of acquittal or the mark of victory, according to certain customs of the time; "a new name" that only the person who receives it knows (because it is the perfect expression of his character) and that will serve as his passport into the kingdom of heaven. "He that hath an ear, let him hear what the Spirit saith unto the churches" (2:22).

Letter to the Church of Thyatira

Of the seven letters to the churches, the one to Thyatira is the longest, the richest as far as content, the most contrasted, and the most dramatic. That is not surprising, because the symbolic church of Thyatira covers some twelve centuries of church history. And what history! That of papal supremacy from AD 538 to 1798.

In 538 Emperor Justinian established by decree the bishop of Rome as "corrector of all heretics," at the same time conferring on him temporal and spiritual authority over the whole of Christendom. And the popes kept this supremacy until 1798, when General Berthier arrested Pius VI and took him into exile by order of Napoleon Bonaparte.

Certain commentators have fixed 1517 as the end of the period of Thyatira—the year when the Reformation began. However, if we admit that the end of one period need not necessarily coincide with the beginning of the next, nothing would prevent Thyatira from terminating in 1798, while the period of Sardis could begin in 1517.

Biblical prophecy gives this period of 1260 years a very special importance, since it is mentioned seven times: twice in the Book of Daniel (7:25; 12:7) and five times in the Revelation (11:2, 3; 12:6, 14; 13:5). Each time, this period describes a time of trouble, of persecution, and of great delusion. A suggested meaning of the name *Thyatira* furthermore confirms this description: sacrifice of victims.

We know very little of either the city or the church of Thyatira. In ancient times Thyatira was noted for its dyeing of cloth in purple and scarlet colors. The Book of Acts refers to it when its author relates the conversion of Lydia, "a seller of purple, of the city of Thyatira" (16:14). This detail itself can symbolize a church in which purple and the scarlet robes of its bishops and cardinals were the fashion. It could also be that Lydia, of whom it is said that she "worshipped God," lived in Thyatira when the Christian church began there.

But let us turn to the letter that the Lord sends to the church. The way Jesus begins it shows immediately the gravity of the situation: "These things saith the Son of God, who hath his eyes like unto a flame of fire, and his feet are like fine brass" (2:18). This is the only time in Revelation that Jesus gives Himself the title of Son of God, with the attributes of divinity: omniscience and omnipotence. It is certainly not without reason. He reveals Himself here as He who sees everything and who treads underfoot all who practice iniquity.

To understand the message to the church of Thyatira we must remember that it is addressed to the Christian community. Hence the nuances and the contrasts. The Lord points out not only its defects, as has been too often the case when we speak of the church during the Middle Ages, but also He gives no other church so much praise. "I know thy works, and charity, and service, and faith, and thy patience, and thy works; and the last to be more than the first" (2:19).

It would be easy to comment on each virtue here set before us, for all are a credit to the church of Thyatira. Christendom's history during these long centuries of obscurantism is rich in examples of love, faith, devotion, patience, and sacrifice. Space does not permit mentioning them here.

The unbiased judgment of Him "who hath his eyes like unto a flame of fire" discerns, alas, many negative aspects also. But still He does it with great care, placing the members of the church of Thyatira in three distinct groups.

First there are the faithful ones who are distinguished by all the Christian virtues mentioned but who tolerate Jezebel.

Second, there is "that woman Jezebel, which calleth herself a prophetess" and who teaches and seduces "my servants to commit fornication, and to eat things sacrificed unto idols" (2:20). Jezebel, queen of Sidon, was the wife of one of Israel's worst kings. She introduced the heathen cult of Baal and Astarte into Israel. Here she personifies the supposedly infallible and all-powerful Papacy.

In Biblical prophecy a woman symbolizes the church. She is either a faithful wife when she follows the teachings of her divine husband (Isaiah 54:5, 6; 2 Corinthians 11:2), or she is an adulterous wife when she follows other teachings (Ezekiel 16:22, 32). The expressions "fornication" and "adultery," here repeated three times, perfectly describe the false teaching, idolatry, and immorality that the symbolic Jezebel endeavored to bring into the church, seducing the very servants of Christ.

Third, there are "the rest in Thatira, as many as have not this doctrine, and which have not known the depths of Satan" (2:24). As in the time of King Ahab and Queen Jezebel, there is among God's people a remnant that has not bowed the knee to false gods and that has rejected the doctrines foreign to God's Word. The history of the church teaches us that there have always been devoted men and women who through the centuries have called for a reform in the church and a return to the teaching of the gospel. We can think of the Waldenses, the Albigenses, the Hussites, the Huguenots, the Moravian brethren, Peter Waldo, Savonarola, Wycliffe, John Huss and Jerome of Prague, and others as well.

To these faithful disciples the Lord says simply: "I will put upon you none other burden. But that which ye have already hold fast till I come" (2:24, 25). The Lord will intervene when He considers it opportune. For the time being, He exercises patience toward the others, even toward Jezebel. "I gave her space to repent," even to "them that commit adultery with her" (2:21, 22). If the trials and tribulations would not lead them to repent, "all the churches shall know that I am he which searcheth the reins and hearts: and I will give unto every one of you according to your works," the Lord says in verse 23.

The letter to Thyatira ends like all the others, with a beautiful promise to those who have fought the good fight of faith and have gained the victory. "And he that overcometh, and keepeth my works unto the end, to him will I give power over the nations: and he shall rule them with a rod of iron; as the vessels of a potter shall they be broken to shivers: even as I received of my Father. And I will give him the morning star" (2:26-28).

In other words, those who remain faithful to the teachings of the Lord despite adverse circumstances will shine amid spiritual darkness like the morning star in the night. And when Christ shall appear in His glory, they will reign with Him. "He that hath an ear, let him hear what the Spirit saith unto the churches" (2:29).

Chapter 5

The Message of Jesus to the Churches of Modern Times

The fifth and the sixth letters deal with the history of the Christian church in modern times: first, the letter to the church of Sardis, the one of the Reformation and Protestantism in general, from 1517 on; then, the letter to the church of Philadelphia, the one of the awakening period at the end of the eighteenth and the beginning of the nineteenth centuries.

Letter to the Church of Sardis

Sardis was the capital city of the Lydian kingdom. It reached its height under the reign of King Croesus in the sixth century BC. Built on a rock over fifteen hundred feet high, it was considered impregnable, except in one point. It was there that Cyrus was able to surprise it as "a thief" in the night (3:3). Sardis was taken a second time under similar circumstances, through lack of vigilance, in the third century BC. Hence the reference, "Be watchful" (3:2).

Besides the proverbial riches of Croesus, Sardis was also noted for its woolen garments which this letter likewise mentions (3:4). Already famous, the city rested on its laurels. In the time of John that which remained was literally dying. From a religious point of view the importance of Sardis was very limited.

We first learn about the church at Sardis in the Book of Revelation. It is certain, however, that its origins reach back to the apostolic era. The walls of a church built in the fourth century can still be seen. Sardis was the seat of a bishop.

"These things saith he that hath the seven Spirits of God, and the seven stars" (3:1). Jesus introduces Himself as

One who has the fullness of the Spirit of God and who, as a result, knows perfectly the situation of the church of Sardis. At the same time He insists on affirming again that He controls the church, since He always has in His right hand the seven stars—symbols of His messengers in each church.

By all accounts the church of Sardis had a good reputation, but the Lord does not allow this to deceive Him. He does not judge by appearances, and He reveals here the truth unsparingly: "I know thy works, that thou hast a name that thou livest, and art dead" (3:1). And what remains is on the point of dying (3:2), just as the city itself was dying when John wrote the letter.

Amazing as it may seem, this is the Lord's estimate on the one hand with respect to the Reformation and on the other with respect to Protestantism in general. Certainly the Reformation was "a song of joy," which is what the name Sardis might mean. The Reformation is still a resounding name today and stands as a synonym of life, of rebirth, and of spiritual awakening. Thanks to it, Christianity discovered the meaning of "living by faith in Jesus Christ."

At the same time, even though Protestantism, which arose out of the Reformation, prides itself on the fame of the latter, the facts are quite different. From the time that the princes took into their hands the Reformation movement, religion became an affair of the state as it was formerly under Constantine. He had created "Christianity." These created "Protestantism." In each kingdom a Christianity like that of its ruler, with all that this implies of politics, was set up along with self-interest, compulsion, intolerance, persecution, and also formalism.

In short, even though official Protestantism as the state religion enjoyed an appearance of spiritual life in many countries, it had either died or was dying. And unless there would be a renewal of watchfulness, what remained would die in its turn. Such is, indeed, the sad truth.

And the Lord gives the reason for it: "For I have not found thy works perfect before God" (3:2). In other words, the Reformers had begun a work that had not been carried on. They had opened the way into the search for truth by returning to the Bible, but their successors had stopped along the way. They did not continue the work of the Reformers. This is why Jesus says that the works of the church of Sardis are incomplete.

"Remember therefore how thou hast received and heard, and hold fast, and repent" (3:3). The remedy Christ proposes is simple: The church must return to the Word of God as in the early days of the Reformation. To remain alive spiritually it is not sufficient to have discovered the source of truth. It is not enough even to take pleasure in listening to God's Word. Unless it is put into practice and kept with persistence, "the care of this world, and the deceitfulness of riches" will ultimately "choke the word," as Jesus explained in His parable of the sower (Matthew 13:22).

Only repentance could bring the church of Sardis back to the abundant life of its beginning. For "if therefore thou shalt not watch, I will come on thee as a thief, and thou shalt not know what hour I will come upon thee" (3:3). There is no threat here of disciplinary action, such as that given to the church of Thyatira. The terms used here are those ordinarily employed to announce the return of Christ. First, the exhortation to watch. Then, the statement of His unexpected coming, like that of a thief, at a time no one knows (see Matthew 24:43; Luke 12:39; 1 Thessalonians 5:2; 2 Peter 3:10; Revelation 16:15).

These references to Jesus' coming also contain a time element. Sardis is the church that ought to have recognized the signs pointing to His return: the Lisbon earthquake in 1755; the Dark Day of May 19, 1780, followed by the night when the moon appeared as blood; and the falling of the stars on November 13, 1833. Jesus had plainly foretold these events, and the Revelation echoes His voice: "There was a great earthquake; and the sun became black as sackcloth of hair, and the moon became as blood; and the stars of heaven fell unto the earth, even as a fig tree casteth her untimely figs, when she is shaken of a mighty wind" (6:12, 13; compare Matthew 24:29).

For lack of vigilance and for not having watched, the church of Sardis would be taken by surprise as was the city in earlier times. But this time the Lord Himself would come "as a thief." The surprise would be so much the greater because Protestantism has not denied the return of Christ but has instead generally ignored the signs announcing the glorious and visible return of Christ.

However, as in all the historical periods of the Christian church, there were also in the church of Sardis "a few . . . which have not defiled their garments" (3:4). The actual word used is *names*, that is, characters, or persons, whose moral behavior was not like that of the church itself. For this reason the Lord promises that "they shall walk with" Him "in white: for they are worthy" (3:4).

Clearly, this honor can come only from the righteousness of Christ, which is obtained by faith. But the white garment, without which no one can enter the hall of the marriage supper of the Lamb (Matthew 22:11-14), is itself made of "fine linen, clean and white . . . [which] is the righteousness of saints" (19:8).

The heart of the Reformation message was justification by faith alone, without works of any kind—a fundamental Christian truth. The error of Protestant theology lies in its conclusion that works were without any value whatever, even from an ethical standpoint. Certainly no one can be saved "by works of righteousness" that he may have done (Titus 3:5). "For by grace are ye saved through faith" (Ephesians 2:8). But "faith without works is dead" (James 2:26). Having ignored this truth, the church of Sardis finally had merely the appearance of life. Only "a few names" knew the reality of the Christian life because "they have not defiled their garments" (3:4). To these Jesus promises the white robe of His righteousness.

Jesus repeats this same promise for the benefit of all who will overcome after the example of these few. "He that overcometh, the same shall be clothed in white raiment" (3:5). Furthermore, the Lord adds: "I will not blot out his name out of the book of life" (3:5). In this book are written the names of all before even they were born, as the psalmist declares (Psalm 139:16). God blots out the names of this and that one only when they reject salvation. For those who, on the other hand, confess the name of Jesus in the world, belongs the certainty of Christ's intercession at the throne of grace: "I will confess his name before my Father, and before his angels" (3:5).

"He that hath an ear, let him hear what the Spirit saith unto the churches" (3:6).

Letter to the Church of Philadelphia

The letter to the church at Philadelphia is certainly the best of the seven letters of Revelation. It is addressed to a small community of believers whose Christian virtues still persist in all their purity. The apt references John makes show that he knew the little town, as well as the church which bore its name.

By reason of its geographical situation Philadelphia still governs access to the route crossing the neighboring mountains. It is a key city: the gate to the eastern plateaus. In the time of John it was a small town of not much importance, but because of its position, it was destined to play a significant missionary role.

Philadelphia takes its name from the expressions of loyalty and fidelity shown by its founder, King Attalus II (159-138 BC) toward his brother Eumenes II. It means "brotherly love." The name perfectly fits the small Christian community that had the distinction of living true Christianity. This is also why Jesus has no reproach for the Philadelphian Christians—no reproach as was the case with the church of Smyrna. Even today the city still has a Christian community with five churches.

From the prophetic point of view Philadelphia represents the church of brotherly love and missionary activity from 1755–1844. Several other dates have been suggested. Here more than elsewhere, precision is difficult, and as has already been said, the beginning of one era does not necessarily correspond to the end of the preceding one. The year 1755 is that of the great Lisbon earthquake, the first sign heralding the nearness of Christ's return (6:12). This earthquake not only shook the earth but also the conscience. Now began the period of the great religious revivals during the second half of the eighteenth and the first half of the nineteenth centuries.

To the church of Philadelphia Jesus introduces Himself with the attributes of divinity: "These things saith he that is holy, he that is true, he that hath the key of David, he that openeth, and no man shutteth; and shutteth, and no man openeth" (3:7). The decay of the church of Sardis produced a swarm of errors and heresies. It was the proper time, then, to continue the work of the Reformation and to lead the church to more holiness and truth. Only He who is holy and true could accomplish this work, for He alone holds "the key of David"—the power of opening or closing the door to the Messianic kingdom of which King David was the type.

Jesus' praise for the church of Philadelphia applies more to what it *is* than to what it *does*. Three exceptional Christian qualities characterize it: (1) "thou hast a little strength," (2) "hast kept my word," and (3) "hast not denied my name" (3:8). The fact of having "little strength" is generally considered as a deficiency. But from a spiritual point of view it is the ideal condition for God's power to be manifested (2 Corinthians 12:9, 10). The Lord can work much better through the channel of His church when it remains faithful to His Word and lives in a manner that glorifies His name.

Three desirable results follow quite naturally from these three exceptional Christian qualities. They are indicated by the words *behold* or *because* that introduce each of them. It is interesting also to note that according to the Greek, Jesus expresses the first in the perfect tense—referring to a reality already fulfilled—and the third in the future tense—concerning an event still to come.

The first result: "Behold, I have set before thee an open door, and no man can shut it" (3:8). The expression "the open door" indicates favorable opportunities for preaching the gospel. The apostle Paul asked his Christian friends to pray for him "that God would open . . . a door of utterance" so that he could "speak the mystery of Christ" (Colossians 4:3; compare Acts 14:27; 1 Corinthians 16:9; 2 Corinthians 2:12).

The period represented by the church of Philadelphia is precisely the one of open doors. Never before had circumstances been more favorable nor possibilities more opportune for taking the gospel to the world. It was certainly a providential time during which the doors of the nations opened to unprecedented missionary activity. Jesus had stated this in His prophetic discourse as one of the most important signs of His soon coming. "And this gospel of the kingdom shall be preached in all the world for a witness unto all nations; and then shall the end come" (Matthew 24:14).

Surprising as it may seem, the French Revolution of 1789 acted as a sort of spark. Its antireligious attitude rebounded and encouraged the unfolding of a great awakening in the heart of Christendom. In different countries, yet at the same time, Bible students concluded that humanity had reached the last phase of history and that the Second Coming was near. To increase the dissemination of the Scriptures, numerous Bible societies were formed. Finally, in the heart of even the weakest Christian groups at the beginning of the nineteenth century a host of missionaries carried the gospel to the ends of the earth. One of the first, William Carey left for India in 1793. Robert Morrison went to China in 1807. Robert Moffat (1816) as well as David Livingstone (1841) pioneered work in Africa. And hundreds of others followed in their footsteps.

The second result: By opening a door the Lord intended to bring into His church those who had not known Him before. "Behold, I will make them of the synagogue of Satan, which say they are Jews, and are not, but do lie; behold, I will make them to come and worship before thy feet, and to know that I have loved thee" (3:9).

Several interpretations have been given to this text. But whether it speaks of false Jews, false Christians, or heathen, the important point is that the Lord makes them sympathetic to the witness of His church. Furthermore the different interpretations are not mutually exclusive. Between 1816 and 1843 a veritable wave of Jews converted to Christianity. At the same time, Christianity experienced a great revival movement that brought abundant fruitage. Then, too, there was the birth of foreign missions to heathen people. Millions of souls, therefore, came to worship at the feet of Christ—thanks to the extraordinary work of the church of brotherly love.

The third result: "Because thou hast kept the word of my patience, I also will keep thee from the hour of temptation, which shall come upon all the world, to try them that dwell upon the earth" (3:10). We have here a direct reference to events at the end of the world as predicted in the Old Testament: "And at that time shall Michael stand up, the great prince which standeth for the children of thy people: and there shall be a time of trouble, such as never was since there was a nation even to that same time" (Daniel 12:1).

Jesus exhorted the church of Philadelphia: "Hold that fast which thou hast, that no man take thy crown" (3:11). As long as the race is not finished, as long as the fight lasts, the crown of victory can at any moment be lost. Jesus' encouragement to persevere is all the more appropriate because He announces His soon return: "I come quickly."

Everything in the letter to the church of Philadelphia appears in groups of three. The writer is presented under three attributes of divinity. The recipient possesses the three Christian qualities that will permit him to accomplish the kind of works the Lord has prepared beforehand for him. Finally, as to the reward, it carries the triple seal of what God promises to the overcomer.

The Spirit's promise harmonizes wonderfully with the character and work of the Christians in the church of Philadelphia. For having been faithful in God's service, the overcomer will become "a pillar in the temple of my God, and he shall go no more out" (3:12). The pillar symbolizes strength, stability, and victory (see Galatians 2:9; 1 Timothy 3:15; Revelation 10:1). "The temple of my God" signifies the presence of God for eternity.

"I will write upon him the name of my God, and the name of the city of my God, which is new Jerusalem, which cometh down out of heaven from my God: and I will write upon him my new name" (3:12). We have noticed that in the Bible a name is always an expression of personality, of character, or it can indicate ownership. To bear the name of God means that God recognizes the overcomer as His son or daughter. To receive the name of the city of God indicates the right of citizenship in the New Jerusalem, where the overcomer will dwell. To have written on him the new name of Jesus means that the overcomer will reflect perfectly Christ's character. He will be like Him because he will see Him as He is (1 John 3:2). He will bear His new name because Jesus will make Himself known to him as He whom "God . . . hath highly exalted . . . and given . . . a name which is above every name" (Philippians 2:9).

"He that hath an ear, let him hear what the Spirit saith unto the churches" (3:13).

Chapter 6

The Message of Jesus to the Church of Today

The seventh letter of Revelation is addressed to the church of Laodicea. In the prophetic sense it represents the last phase in the history of Christ's church. The Bible calls this period "the last days" or "the time of the end." The letter particularly interests us, since we live in these times and since this last message of Christ to His church is directed to us.

Whatever the meaning given to the name Laodicea—"a judged people," "judgment of the people," "separation of the people," or "rejection of the people"—it is always in relation to the final work of the church. Therefore the period represented by Laodicea began in 1844 at the beginning of the investigative judgment (see Daniel 8:14). We shall return to more details of this prophecy in a later chapter.

The city of Laodicea bore the name of the wife of Antiochus II, its founder (third century BC), and was situated about forty miles southeast of Philadelphia. Its prosperity came to a height in the Roman era from the second century to the first century BC. One of its specialties was working with lustrous black wool. A school of oculists there enjoyed a certain renown in the Greco-Roman world, especially because of an ointment made from Phrygian rocks ground to powder. Laodicea was also a city of banks and businesses.

Two other points are significant. The first is in connection with Christ's reference to the lukewarmness of the church of Laodicea. An aqueduct carried hot water from the springs of Hierapolis, only about six miles away, and delivered it lukewarm to Laodicea. The second illustrates its self-sufficiency. In AD 60, only thirty years before John wrote this letter, Laodicea suffered a devastating earthquake. Rome offered monetary aid, but the inhabitants refused, saying that they had need of nothing.

At the time when Paul wrote his letter to the Colossians, probably around AD 62, there was already a church in Laodicea. Apparently Paul never visited there (Colossians 2:1), and probably Epaphras, originally from Colosse, was its founder (Colossians 1:7; 4:12). Paul wrote to the church of Laodicea at the same time he sent one to the church of Colosse (4:16). Some scholars think that it was simply a copy of the epistle sent to the Ephesians.

Laodicea survived until the thirteenth century, when the Turks destroyed it. Today only ruins are left at the original site, but the message that carries its name has retained its importance, for it directly concerns us. Therefore we should lend a particularly attentive ear to Christ's words.

Jesus introduces Himself to His last church in a very appropriate manner. He is the personification of the "Amen," that is, the "Yes" of God in whom His word is completely fulfilled. He is true, steadfast, and trustworthy. The history of His church both begins and ends with Him. He is, therefore, well named "Alpha and Omega, the beginning and the end, the first and the last" (22:13; see 1:8).

The second title helps the first one. As "the faithful and true witness" Jesus is the perfect expression of God's thought, will, and character. As a New Testament author puts it, He is "the brightness of his glory, and the express image of his person" (Hebrews 1:3). "For in him dwelleth all the fulness of the Godhead bodily" (Colossians 2:9).

Finally, Jesus reveals Himself to the church of Laodicea as being "the beginning of the creation of God" (3:14). Some have concluded from this that Christ was the first of God's creatures. The Greek word here can be translated also as "the first cause," which is something altogether different. Christ is presented here as the principle, the first cause, of God's creation—He by whom "all things were made" (John 1:3).

The Christians of Laodicea certainly understood John's

meaning, for they had already read Paul's solemn declaration: "For by him were all things created, that are in
heaven, and that are in earth, visible and invisible,
whether they be thrones, or dominions, or principalities,
or powers: all things were created by him, and for him: and
he is before all things, and by him all things consist" (Colossians 1:16, 17; compare Hebrews 1:1-3). Christ's role as
Creator is appropriate to the message of the time of judgment. It lifts the vision immediately to the dimensions of
the universe.

Under these three titles Jesus introduces Himself as the
One in whom God's will is always completely fulfilled, the
One who is the perfect image of the invisible God, and the
One by whom God created and sustains the universe. Cer-
tainly these provide sufficient reason for taking very seri-
ously the Lord's counsel to Christians of the last days.

"I know thy works, that thou art neither cold nor hot"
(3:15). Contrary to His practice, the Lord does not give one
word of praise concerning the works of Laodicea. Instead,
Jesus puts His finger directly on the problem, which is not
doctrinal or ecclesiastical but entirely spiritual: lukewarmness and self-satisfaction.

"I would thou wert cold or hot" (3:15). Nothing is more
loathsome than a half-and-half Christian. "Halfhearted
Christians are worse than infidels; for their deceptive
words and noncommittal position lead many astray. The
infidel shows his colors. The lukewarm Christian deceives
both parties. He is neither a good worldling nor a good
Christian. Satan uses him to do a work that no one else can
do" (Ellen G. White, *Seventh-day Adventist Bible Commentary*, Vol. 7, p. 963).

Spiritual lukewarmness, like tepid water, produces
nausea, but God's words are a warning, not an irrevocable
decision. The verbal form of the Greek underlines the conditional character of the statement. Other translations give
the idea very well by saying: "I am going to spit you out"
(TEV*), or "I shall [have to] spue you out" (e.g., The River-

*From The Bible in Today's English Version. Copyright, American
Bible Society, 1976.

side New Testament). As in the time of the prophet Elijah, the Lord puts a radical choice before Christians of the last days. He will not allow them indefinitely to "halt . . . between two opinions" (1 Kings 18:21). This is also why the work of Elijah typifies the work that must be done at the time of the end (Malachi 4:5, 6).

The fundamental reason for the lukewarm condition is revealed in the judgment of self-sufficiency: "Because thou sayest, I am rich, and increased with goods, and have need of nothing . . ." (3:17). This statement can be understood in both a literal and a symbolic sense. The city of Laodicea did not lack riches, nor are they lacking today in our so-called Christian society. Likewise the treasure of God's Word has never been more accessible. Presently the Bible enjoys a worldwide circulation as does no other book. Never has it been more studied and commented upon, thus fulfilling the prophecy that says in "the time of the end: many shall run to and fro, and knowledge shall be increased" (Daniel 12:4). Its riches are at anyone's disposal, and the temptation exists for the contemporary Christian world to say of itself: "I am rich, and increased with goods, and have need of nothing."

But to rest satisfied with one's riches, even spiritual riches, constitutes a real danger. From the moment that one no longer recognizes them as gifts of God but takes merit to oneself, self-sufficiency blinds the eyes of even the most clear-thinking individual. In their blindness modern Laodiceans simply think that they no longer need the treasures of God's Word, nor sometimes even God Himself. Have not certain contemporary theologians gone so far as to talk about the death of God and about a Christianized atheism? To think oneself rich means losing the measure of what is divine, because the kingdom of heaven is for those who by the Spirit know that they are poor (as the Christians of the church of Smyrna in Revelation 2:9) but who, however, have enriched the world (Matthew 5:3; 2 Corinthians 6:10).

The church of Laodicea lives in a culture completely remote from reality. What it is and what it does is the opposite of what it professes to be. The real picture as the

Lord sees it reveals the most tragic of spiritual conditions. Thou "knowest not that thou art wretched, and miserable, and poor, and blind, and naked" (3:17). In fact, it is not that the Laodiceans are hypocrites but rather that they are lamentably ignorant of their actual spiritual condition. This is why, having revealed their evil, the Lord prescribes the remedy.

The very fact, however, that He gives an exhortation shows that the situation is not incurable. Certainly the evil is serious and demands urgent attention. Nevertheless, although the reproaches are direct, the exhortations are full of tenderness. The proposed remedies are progressive. First, there is counsel. Second, if He needs to, God will act as a father to His son by correcting him. Third, the Lord will use persuasion and will intervene personally if necessary.

Among these recommended remedies are various objects of value and of local trade in the city of Laodicea: gold, clothing, and ointment. They also symbolize that which Jesus alone can provide. "I counsel thee to buy of me," He offers (3:18). The verb *buy* is the exact word for these bargainers, as it is also the appropriate one for our generation whose characteristic surely is business (Luke 17:28). However, He does not mean that one must buy with money, but simply that we must arrange to exchange our deceptive values for the unspeakable values of Christ (Isaiah 55:1). Even though salvation is free, it always costs a tremendous amount to arrive at the point of considering "the reproach of Christ greater riches than the treasures in Egypt" (Hebrews 11:26).

"Gold tried in the fire" (3:18) is the first treasure Jesus recommends. It is a symbol of faith working by love (1 Peter 1:7; James 2:5). Spiritual riches are here contrasted with the riches of the Laodicean bankers. "It makes the heart rich; for it has been purged until it is pure, and the more it is tested the more brilliant is its luster" (*Testimonies for the Church*, Vol. 4, p. 88).

"The white raiment" offered by Jesus is contrasted with the garments of black wool that were a specialty of Laodicean trade. They symbolize the righteousness of Christ given to every repentant sinner so that he may "be clothed,

and that the shame of" his "nakedness do not appear"
(3:18). "The white raiment is purity of character, the righteousness of Christ imparted to the sinner. This is indeed a
garment of heavenly texture, that can be bought only of
Christ for a life of willing obedience" (ibid.). Without this
garment no one can be admitted to the marriage feast of the
Lamb (Matthew 22:11-14). That is why John wrote:
"Blessed are they that wash their robes, that they may have
right to the tree of life, and may enter in through the gates
into the city" (Revelation 22:14, margin).

Finally, to cure the Laodiceans of their spiritual blindness, Jesus offers them an "eyesalve" so that they can see.
Since this deals with caring for spiritual vision, it refers to
the conscience or the inward eye, the light of the soul
(Matthew 6:22, 23). It will make clear the real conditions of
wretchedness and spiritual poverty in the church. Only by
the anointing of the Holy Spirit, the divine eyesalve, can
Jesus enlighten the eyes of our understanding (Ephesians
1:18) and make the light shine in our hearts (2 Corinthians
4:6).

"The eyesalve is that wisdom and grace which enables
us to discern between the evil and the good, and to detect
sin under any guise. God has given His church eyes which
He requires them to anoint with wisdom, that they may see
clearly" (ibid., pp. 88, 89).

However, if the church of Laodicea remains indifferent
to the counsel of Jesus by neglecting His advice, in His love
for her He will not hesitate to use trial. For, He says, "As
many as I love, I rebuke and chasten" (3:19). Divine instruction is always dictated by love.

Greek has three different words for the various love
relationships that can exist between God and man, and
between man and man. The first, which the New Testament writers do not use, is *eros*, or erotic love—sensual and
selfish. At the other extreme is *agapē*, the love defined by
Paul in 1 Corinthians 13 and which he calls "the bond of
perfectness" (Colossians 3:14). This love is based on respect
and honor. It is neither feeling, nor sentiment, even less
passion, but it is a principle of action. Finally, between
these two there is *philia*, affectionate love—friendly, frater-

nal, based on emotion and feeling (2 Peter 1:7).

Now it is specifically this affectionate, fraternal love that the Lord has for the church of Laodicea, in contrast to the *agapē* love manifested to the church of Philadelphia (3:9). The spiritual conditions justify this difference. It is always as a friend and brother that the Lord rebukes and chastens all whom He loves.

At first He rebukes in order to make us aware that we have faults and that our spiritual condition is not what it should be. Then He wishes to "correct," "educate," or "discipline," as it is possible to translate the verb used here. Jesus has one aim only: to make all those who allow themselves to be fashioned by Him genuine children of God. That is why He makes the imperative appeal: "Be zealous therefore, and repent" (3:19).

After counsel comes warning, for the Lord awaits a positive result—unless Laodicea "despisest . . . the riches of his goodness and forbearance and longsuffering; not knowing that the goodness of God leadeth . . . to repentance" (Romans 2:4). To be zealous means to be hot. What the Lord wanted from Laodicea, He now demands in the imperative mood. Only true repentance—a radical change in the manner of thinking, of speaking, and of doing—can lead to this goal.

It is not a question of wanting the good: "For to will is present with me; but how to perform that which is good I find not," cried the apostle Paul. "O wretched man that I am! who shall deliver me from the body of this death? I thank God through Jesus Christ our Lord" (Romans 7:18, 24, 25). Jesus said: "Without me ye can do nothing" (John 15:5). And so, overflowing with love for Laodicea, the Lord comes in person, face-to-face, to offer His help.

"Behold, I stand at the door and knock: if any man hear my voice, and open the door, I will come in to him, and will sup with him, and he with me" (3:20). Jesus stands at the door! He is outside because He has been put outside and has been left outside. But like a humble peddler going from door to door, He offers His cures to whoever will open to Him, for the door can only be opened from inside. Someone must hear His voice. What love, what solicitude, what respect for man's freedom! Everybody can be saved, but nobody will be saved in spite of himself. Only the one who hears His voice and who opens the door to let Him come in will know communion with Christ, symbolized by the supper, without which there is no true spiritual life.

Although the mystical interpretation of this passage seems to force itself upon us, we should not exclude the eschatological one. The expression "I stand at the door" clearly echoes Jesus' announcement of His imminent return in glory: "So likewise ye, when ye shall see all these things, know that it is near, even at the doors" (Matthew 24:33; see also Luke 12:36; James 5:9). Even the reference to supper recalls the meal that the elect will enjoy with their Saviour in the kingdom of heaven on the day of the marriage feast of the Lamb.

The letter to the church of Laodicea closes, as do the others, with a promise: "To him that overcometh will I grant to sit with me in my throne, even as I also overcame, and am set down with my Father in his throne" (3:21). Christ's promise directly relates with what precedes, and it resembles what Jesus had said earlier to His disciples. "And I appoint unto you a kingdom, as my Father hath appointed unto me; that ye may eat and drink at my table in my kingdom, and sit on thrones judging the twelve tribes of Israel" (Luke 22:29, 30).

Christ's promise is a logical conclusion to this letter as well as to the group of seven letters. The cycle finishes, therefore, with the victory of Christ and His church. All those who will have fought a good fight, finished the course, and kept the faith will be able to say with Paul: "Henceforth there is laid up for me a crown of righteousness, which the Lord, the righteous judge, shall give me at that day: and not to me only, but unto all them also that love his appearing" (2 Timothy 4:8).

For the last time, the Lord repeats once more this sentence which remains unchanged: "He that hath an ear, let him hear what the Spirit saith unto the churches" (3:22). Nothing emphasizes more the importance of hearing in the work of salvation. If man had been smitten with blindness as a result of sin, there would still remain the possibility of

hearing God's voice, provided he lent a listening ear. The
wisdom of the child of God consists not in judging but in
listening. Jesus said, "Blessed is he that readeth, and they
that hear the words of this prophecy, and keep those which
are written therein: for the time is at hand" (1:3).

Jesus' messages to the seven churches certainly do have
a historical application. But in one way or another they
concern all who wish to live in Christ and triumph by His
grace. Especially, however, "the message to the Laodicean
church is applicable to our condition. How plainly is pic-
tured the position of those who think they have all the
truth, who take pride in their knowledge of the Word of
God, while its sanctifying power has not been felt in their
lives. The fervor of the love of God is wanting in their
hearts, but it is this very fervor of love that makes God's
people the light of the world" (Ellen G. White, *The
Seventh-day Adventist Bible Commentary*, Vol. 7, p. 961).

Chapter 7

"Knowing the Time"

Christ's message to the church of Laodicea is a ringing appeal for Christians of our time to "live soberly, righteously, and godly, in this present world; looking for that blessed hope, and the glorious appearing of the great God and our Saviour Jesus Christ" (Titus 2:12, 13). And Paul encourages the faithful in Rome with the same idea, "that, knowing the time, that now it is high time to awake out of sleep: for now is our salvation nearer than when we believed. The night is far spent, the day is at hand" (Romans 13:11, 12).

Particular prophecies have been given, and numerous signs of the times allow the Bible scholar, just as the prophets did previously, to recognize "what manner of time the Spirit of Christ which was in them did signify, when it testified beforehand the sufferings of Christ, and the glory that should follow" (1 Peter 1:11).

Alas! Today, as in the time of Jesus, we know better how to forecast tomorrow's weather than to discern the signs of the times. "When it is evening, ye say, It will be fair weather: for the sky is red. And in the morning, It will be foul weather to day: for the sky is red and lowring, O ye hypocrites, ye can discern the face of the sky; but can ye not discern the signs of the times?" (Matthew 16:2, 3).

Jesus directed this rebuke at the Pharisees and the Sadducees who, to tempt Him, had asked Him for "a sign from heaven." Such an approach revealed the blindness of Israel's religious leaders, for they had just seen a convincing public demonstration of Jesus' Messiahship.

The evangelist relates the miracles performed on this occasion as being Messianic signs proclaimed by the prophecy: "They saw the dumb to speak, the maimed to be whole, the lame to walk, and the blind to see," and "the multitude wondered," "and they glorified the God of Israel" (Matthew 15:31). To seal this demonstration, Jesus crowned it all by one of His most extraordinary miracles—the multiplication of the loaves and fishes.

It is in this context that Jesus' question is placed: "Can ye not discern the signs of the times?" The expression "the signs of the times" has in our day become part of current speech, but the sense given it today rarely relates to Biblical prophecy. When we say that blue jeans, hitchhiking, drugs, or kidnapping is "a sign of the times," we simply mean that these characterize the century, the period, or the year.

For Jesus and His contemporaries, this expression had another meaning. First of all, it had a prophetic significance. It referred to specific signs announced by the prophets that made it possible to recognize the time of the Messiah. Because these signs marked historical time, they had a chronological value.

This was the evangelist's meaning when he related the events that had led Jesus to speak of the signs of the times. But if the religious leaders did not want to recognize them as such, the crowds were not mistaken about them. "Then those men, when they had seen the miracle that Jesus did, said, This is of a truth that prophet that should come into the world" (John 6:14). And drawing what appeared to them to be the logical conclusion, they prepared to proclaim Jesus king (verse 15).

Asking for an additional sign from heaven, therefore, proved the unbelief of Israel's religious leaders and their inability to understand the prophetic import of Messiah's words and deeds. Hence the comment of Jesus: "Ye can discern the face of the sky; but can ye not discern the signs of the times?" To which He added: "A wicked and adulterous generation seeketh after a sign; and there shall no sign be given unto it, but the sign of the prophet Jonas" (Matthew 16:4).

His allusion to Jonah gave an additional sign by which even a wicked and adulterous generation could recognize

His Messiahship. "For as Jonas was three days and three nights in the whale's belly; so shall the Son of man be three days and three nights in the heart of the earth" (Matthew 12:40). In other words, Jesus' death and resurrection was the sign that He gave to His adversaries.

The prophetic word that Jesus Himself used after His resurrection to open the understanding of His disciples not only gives us the signs by which we can recognize Jesus as the promised Messiah (Luke 24:25), prophecy also provides us with signs that permit us to fix the time of His ministry. And what holds true for the first advent of Jesus is equally true for the Second Advent.

In fact, did not God reveal to the prophet Daniel the exact time of Messiah's coming and death? "Seventy weeks are determined upon thy people and upon thy holy city, to finish the transgression, and to make an end of sins, and to make reconciliation for iniquity, and to bring in everlasting righteousness, and to seal up the vision and prophecy, and to anoint the most Holy" (Daniel 9:24). This is how the work of the Messiah is described at the end of the seventy prophetic weeks. As to His death, it is fixed in the middle of the last week: "After threescore and two weeks shall Messiah be cut off, and shall have nothing: . . . and in the midst of the week he shall cause the sacrifice and the oblation to cease" (verses 26, margin, 27).

In the time of Jesus most everyone in Israel expected the Messiah to come. "The people were in expectation, and all men mused in their hearts of John, whether he were the Christ, or not" (Luke 3:15). The leaders of the Jews even sent a delegation to John the Baptist to ask him if he was "that prophet," that is, the expected Messiah. John replied without any possible equivocation that he was only "the voice of one crying in the wilderness, Make straight the way of the Lord." He added immediately: "But there standeth one among you, whom ye know not; . . . who coming after me, . . . whose shoe's latchet I am not worthy to unloose" (John 1:23, 26, 27).

From the beginning of His ministry Jesus Himself proclaimed that the time of the Messiah had come: "The time is *fulfilled,** and the kingdom of God is at hand: repent ye, and believe the gospel" (Mark 1:15). That Jesus had come at the appropriate time Paul affirmed several times in his epistles: *"When the fulness of the time was come,* God sent forth his Son, made of a woman, made under the law" (Galatians 4:4). And speaking of the plan of redemption, he explained that God had "made known unto us the mystery of his will, according to his good pleasure which he hath purposed in himself: that in the dispensation of *the fulness of times* he might gather together in one all things in Christ" (Ephesians 1:9, 10).

Jesus Himself certainly had an understanding of the prophecies of Daniel, one of which He quotes in Matthew 24:15. He certainly also knew that His ministry would last only for the time predicted by the prophetic word— namely, three and a half years. Is this why He fearlessly replied to His disciples, who were terrified by the threats of the Jews against Him: "My time is not yet come. . . . Go ye up unto this feast: I go not up yet unto this feast; for *my time is not yet full come"* (John 7:6-8)? However, on the eve of His arrest Jesus did not hesitate to pray: "Father, the hour is come" (John 17:1). And the evangelist noted that "Jesus knew that his hour was come that he should depart out of this world unto the Father" (13:1).

If God could so make known the time of Christ's first advent, it could certainly be the same in respect to His second coming. And so we must attentively study "the signs of the times," for this expression also has an eschatological meaning, announcing the coming in glory of the Lord Jesus Christ. Following the prophet Daniel, Jesus and the apostles called this time "the time of the end," "the end of the times," or simply "the end" or "the last days."

Several times we find in the Book of Daniel expressions like these: "Understand, O son of man: for at *the time of the end* shall be the vision" (8:17); "For at the *time appointed the end shall be"* (8:19); and "The end shall be *at the time appointed"* (11:27; compare verse 35). Finally to the prophet, who was anxious to understand the meaning of his visions,

---

*Emphasis in Bible texts is supplied by author.

it was said "But thou, O Daniel, shut up the words, and seal the book, *even to the time of the end:* many shall run to and fro, and knowledge shall be increased" (12:4). When the prophet insisted that he did not understand, the same declaration was made a second time: "Go thy way, Daniel: for the words are closed up and sealed till *the time of the end.* . . . The wise shall understand" (12:9, 10).

Scripture, then, speaks of a time appointed for the end. Consequently the signs of the times should allow us to identify the period. Without entering into a detailed explanation of numerical prophecy as it relates to the time of the end, let us note that the expression "time, times, and a half" or its equivalent is repeated seven times: twice in Daniel (7:25; 12:7), and five times in Revelation (11:2, 3; 12:6, 14; 13:5). This shows the importance that Scripture places on this time period.

In order to make it easily understood, Scripture gives the numerical value in three different forms: 1260 days, 42 months, and three and a half years. According to the principle of a prophetic day being equal to a literal year (see Ezekiel 4:6), this means 1260 literal years. An additional detail particularly emphasizes time: The wording "a *time,* and *times,* and half a *time.*"

The details in Daniel 7 make it quite clear that this important prophecy applies to that period of history symbolized by the little horn, which corresponds to the 1260 years of papal supremacy. It began some time during the Roman Empire but after the barbarian invasions had divided the empire into ten parts. During this time civil power gave way to religious power.

The Apocalypse summarizes this transfer of power with these words: "The dragon gave him his power, and his seat, and great authority. . . . And power was given unto him to continue forty and two months" (13:2-5). This event took place in AD 538, after which the popes took in hand the destiny of the western Roman Empire. The 1260 years of this prophecy ended in 1798 when General Berthier of the French Revolution entered Rome and led Pope Pius VI into exile.

The year 1798 is, therefore, an important prophetic date,

since it marks both the end of the temporal power of the pope and the beginning of "the time of the end." Daniel had been told to shut up the words of his prophecies and to seal his book "even to the time of the end: many shall run to and fro, and knowledge shall be increased" (Daniel 12:4).

In counterreaction to the antireligious attitude of the French Revolution, many students of the Bible in various countries began to examine the prophecies, especially those of Daniel and the Revelation. Their research led them to conclude that humanity had entered the last phase of its history and that the second coming of Jesus was near. The result was the great nineteenth-century religious movement known as the Advent Awakening.

In certain cases some have made the mistake of fixing a date, a day, or an hour that they believed to be the time of Jesus' return. They had forgotten the words of the Master which specified that it is not given to us "to know the times or the seasons, which the Father hath put in his own power" and which He alone knows (Acts 1:7; see Matthew 24:36). However, does this mean that we must adopt the widespread attitude of complete indifference to knowing the times—the same attitude maintained by the religious leaders in the time of Jesus?

There is an essential difference between trying to know the day and the hour of Christ's return and seeking to discern the signs connected with His return. Jesus Himself makes this distinction in His prophetic discourse. Athough on the one hand He refuses to give the least indication as to the day and the hour of His return, on the other hand He multiplies the signs whereby we can discern the nearness of His coming. Moreover, this discourse is a direct response to a particular question asked by His disciples: "Tell us, *when* shall these things be? and what shall be the *sign* of thy coming, and of the end of the world?" (Matthew 24:3; see also Luke 21:7).

Some of His disciples had just praised the beauty of the temple, and Jesus said to them: "See ye not all these things? verily I say unto you, There shall not be left here one stone upon another, that shall not be thrown down" (Matthew 24:2). Then having gone up to the Mount of Olives, where a panoramic view of the whole city could be seen, Jesus traced in broad outline the events indicative of the end of Jerusalem and of the end of the world.

We shall not linger over the numerous signs given by Jesus in this discourse. One only will occupy our attention, the one that especially deals with time. Even in our days it constitutes a critical point in the political world: Jerusalem. In fact, Jerusalem is both the beginning and the culmination of Jesus' prophecy. For Him, as for Daniel the prophet, the history of nations, as that of the people of Israel, is written in the setting of the tragic history of Jerusalem. The latter is the sign by which the fate of the former is determined. So having predicted the destruction of Jerusalem and the dispersion of the Jews "into all nations," Jesus declared, "Jerusalam shall be trodden down of the Gentiles, *until the times of the Gentiles be fulfilled*" (Luke 21:24).

Few today would deny the precision of this prophecy. The destruction of Jerusalem by the Roman armies in AD 70 is a historical fact commemorated on the triumphal arch of Titus in Rome. The dispersion of the Jews among all nations is still a reality. As for Jerusalem, nineteen centuries of history should provide adequate proof that it has been "trodden down of the Gentiles"—first by the Romans, then by the Arabs, next by different Christian nations during the Crusades, fourth by the Turks up to the end of the first world war, then by the British, and finally by the Jordanians until the Six-Day War in June, 1967.

This prophecy of Jesus was a sign for the Christians of the Apostolic Church, who lived at the beginning of the times of the Gentiles, and it remains a sign for us who live at the end of the times of the Gentiles. Again, we must know how to discern its meaning.

It is not a matter of our seeing in the return of the Jews to Palestine and in the Israeli conquest of Jerusalem a sign of the approaching conversion of the Jews, as so many Christians think. Nothing in Jesus' prophecy allows such an interpretation. However, if we cannot see that Jerusalem is an exceptional sign of the times, then might we not be placing ourselves in the same position as the religious leaders who knew how to "discern the face of the sky" but could not discern the obvious "signs of the times"?

In order for us to understand Jesus' statement, three questions need answering. First, what exactly does the expression "the times of the Gentiles" mean? Then, what should be understood by the fulfillment of the times of the Gentiles? Finally, what connection is there between the retaking of Jerusalem by the Jews and the fulfillment of the times of the Gentiles?

As I understand the Biblical language, the times of the Gentiles is the period set aside by God for the evangelization of the heathen nations. It is not the time needed for them to be converted to Christianity, as some think, but for them to hear the gospel. It is in this sense that Jesus said: "This gospel of the kingdom shall be preached in all the world for a witness unto all nations; and then shall the end come" (Matthew 24:14).

I believe that the times of the Gentiles began in AD 34, when the prophetic seventy weeks that God set aside for the people of Israel ended. The baptism of the first "heathens"—the Ethiopian eunuch and the centurion Cornelius—as well as the conversion of Paul as the apostle to the Gentiles mark the beginning of these new times when the gospel would be preached to the nations. And if I have understood the prediction of Jesus properly, this time will be "fulfilled" when Jerusalem will cease to "be trodden down of the Gentiles." The fact that since 1967 Gentiles no longer have occupied Jerusalem means, therefore, that we are now living at the end of "the times of the Gentiles."

Jerusalem here constitutes the last sign of the times by which the Lord shows us that the history of this world is coming to its climax and that the restoration of all things is at hand. And should God tarry once more in the fulfillment of His promise, we should understand that He "is longsuffering, . . . not willing that any should perish, but that all should come to repentance" (2 Peter 3:9).

Chapter 8

The Hour of Judgment

Referring to some people's attitude with regard to the teaching of the Lord and of the apostles, Peter declared: "In the last days . . . they willingly are ignorant" of the Biblical teaching concerning the creation of the world, of the Flood story, of the prophecies dealing with the end, of the promise that Christ would return, and of the judgment of God (2 Peter 3:3-7).

Certainly it is quite possible to be ignorant of all this, even of God Himself—as many are in our own day. But men will never succeed in eradicating the idea of justice that is deeply rooted in their conscience. But to speak of justice presupposes a judgment. The prickings of conscience and the terror of death are obvious proofs that human beings expect to give account at some time or other and in one way or another. The religious ceremonies of all peoples since hoary antiquity abundantly testify to this. Now what we sense instinctively, the Scriptures teach clearly.

All the teaching of the Old Testament on the subject of the judgment is condensed in the statement: "Fear God, and keep his commandments: for this is the whole duty of man. For God shall bring every work into judgment, with every secret thing, whether it be good, or whether it be evil" (Ecclesiastes 12:13, 14).

Echoing the same thought, the apostle Paul wrote to the Corinthians that "we must all appear before the judgment seat of Christ; that every one may receive the things done in his body, according to that he hath done, whether it be good or bad" (2 Corinthians 5:10). And in his speech on Mars Hill to the learned men of Athens he declared that "the times of this ignorance God winked at; but now commandeth all men every where to repent: because he hath appointed a day, in the which he will judge the world in righteousness by that man whom he hath ordained; whereof he hath given assurance unto all men, in that he hath raised him from the dead" (Acts 17:30, 31).

The idea of a judgment at a specific time destroys at a stroke the widespread belief of an individual judgment immediately after death that decides the eternal reward or punishment. On the contrary, the sacred writers place the judgment in the future. "When I shall find the set time I will judge uprightly," says the Lord (Psalm 75:2, margin). "God shall judge the righteous and the wicked" (Ecclesiastes 3:17). "Therefore judge nothing before the time, until the Lord come, who both will bring to light the hidden things of darkness, and will make manifest the counsels of the hearts" (1 Corinthians 4:5). Reporting a discourse of Paul, Luke wrote that "he reasoned of righteousness, temperance, and judgment to come" (Acts 24:25).

Jesus Himself did not speak differently. When He referred to judgment He placed it in the future: "But I say unto you, it shall be more tolerable for Tyre and Sidon at the day of judgment, than for you" (Matthew 11:22). "But I say unto you, That every idle word that men shall speak, they shall give account thereof in the day of judgment. For by thy words thou shalt be justified, and by thy words thou shalt be condemned" (Matthew 12:36, 37).

It follows, therefore, that the judgment will take place at the conclusion of human history. Everybody without exception must appear before the judgment seat of Christ. Everyone's works will be judged. God "will render to every man according to his deeds: to them who by patient continuance in well doing seek for glory and honour and immortality, eternal life; but unto them that are contentious, and do not obey the truth, but obey unrighteousness, indignation and wrath" (Romans 2:6-8).

A more careful examination of the different texts that mention the judgment allows us to distinguish three successive phases of it, somewhat as in a civil trial. There is first of all the hearing, or the investigation of the case, during which the fate of each one is decided. Then comes the announcement of the verdict and the penalty for the wicked, during the millennium. Finally there is the execution of the sentence, after the millennium.

Our interest here will concentrate on the first part of the judgment, that which we conveniently call the investigative judgment. The eternal destiny of each individual depends on it. That is why the Lord also gives it a special importance, because our understanding of prophecy indicates that since 1844 "the hour of his judgment is come" (Revelation 14:7).

The Book of Daniel devotes a place of prime importance to the investigative judgment. In fact, Daniel paints a thrilling picture of the inaugural scene, at the same time placing it in the chronological order of unfolding history. "I beheld till the thrones were placed, and the Ancient of days did sit, whose garment was white as snow, and the hair of his head like the pure wool: his throne was like the fiery flame, and his wheels as burning fire. A fiery stream issued and came forth from before him: thousand thousands ministered unto him, and ten thousand times ten thousand stood before him: the judgment was set, and the books were opened" (7:9, 10, margin).

In the account of the vision itself and in the interpretation given to it, there are two time factors of the highest importance. First, this judgment scene takes place *before* the appearing of "the Son of man . . . with the clouds of heaven," so that the earthly powers' "lives were prolonged for a season and time" (Daniel 7:13, 12). Second, this phase of the judgment immediately follows the fulfillment of the 1260-year prophecy in 1798. "The saints . . . shall be given into his hand until a time and times and the dividing of time. But the judgment shall sit" (Daniel 7:25, 26).

Wishing to clarify things for those living at the time of the end, the Lord entrusted to Daniel the longest time prophecy. It is found in Daniel 8 and was given to complete the preceding chapter. It answers the questions: "How long shall be the vision concerning the daily sacrifice, and the transgression of desolation, to give both the sanctuary and the host to be trodden under foot?" by stating, "Unto two thousand and three hundred days; then shall the sanctuary be cleansed" (verses 13, 14).

Daniel wanted to understand the vision, so the angel Gabriel came expressly to tell him that it dealt with "the time of the end" (verse 17). "For at the time appointed the end shall be" (verse 19), he specified. Then the angel concluded by saying: "And the vision of the evening and the morning which was told is true: wherefore shut thou up the vision; for it shall be for many days" (verse 26).

It is not surprising, then, that we had to wait until the beginning of the nineteenth century to understand the vision of the 2300 evenings and mornings. It had remained sealed "even to the time of the end," as had been stated to Daniel (12:4). But when God considered the time to be ripe, He revealed the secret of the vision to those who pondered over it.

Until the second half of the eighteenth century, it was not clear how to interpret the 2300-day prophecy. Then Johann P. Petri, a reform pastor in Germany, concluded that the seventy weeks and the 2300 days had the same starting point. All that remained was to find the exact date for "the going forth of the commandment to restore and to build Jerusalem" (Daniel 9:25). On this point commentators have differed, but Adventists generally agree that Artaxerxes I authorized the rebuilding in 457 BC. Consequently, the year 1844 ends the prophecy of the 2300 evenings and mornings.

"It is both interesting and significant that more than sixty men in the early nineteenth century, scattered over four continents, and located in twelve different countries—including even a Roman Catholic supreme court justice, José de Rozas of Mexico City—looked to 1843, '44, or '47 as the terminus of this epochal period. And nearly all of them published their expectations *before William Miller's first book appeared in Troy, New York, in 1836"* (*Questions on Doctrine,* p. 314).

We know the part William Miller played not only in connection with the time 1843-44 but especially concerning the significance of the event predicted. "Miller and his associates proclaimed that the longest and last prophetic period brought to view in the Bible was about to expire, that the judgment was at hand, and the everlasting kingdom was to be ushered in. . . .

"In explaining Daniel 8:14, 'Unto two thousand and three hundred days; then shall the sanctuary be cleansed,' Miller . . . adopted the generally received view that the earth is the sanctuary, and he believed that the cleansing of the sanctuary represented the purification of the earth by fire at the coming of the Lord. When, therefore, he found that the close of the 2300 days was definitely foretold, he concluded that this revealed the time of the second advent. His error resulted from accepting the popular view as to what constitutes the sanctuary" (*The Great Controversy*, pp. 351, 352).

In order to understand the meaning of the expression "then shall the sanctuary be cleansed," we should refer to the services of the earthly sanctuary, which are a figure or a shadow of the heavenly sanctuary (Hebrews 8:5; 9:9, 11, 23, 24). These services were of two kinds: the daily service and the yearly one. Christ's intercession as our High Priest was symbolized by the daily service, whereas the yearly service on the Day of Atonement foreshadowed Christ's work at the end of time.

"The cleansing of the sanctuary was the last service performed by the high priest in the yearly round of ministration. It was the closing work of the atonement—a removal or putting away of sin from Israel. It prefigured the closing work in the ministration of our High Priest in heaven, in the removal or blotting out of the sins of His people, which are registered in the heavenly records."

"But before this can be accomplished, there must be an examination of the books of record to determine who, through repentance of sin and faith in Christ, are entitled to the benefits of His atonement. The cleansing of the sanctuary therefore involves a work of investigation—a work of judgment. This work must be performed prior to the coming of Christ to redeem His people; for when He comes, His reward is with Him to give to every man according to his works. Revelation 22:12" (*ibid.*, pp. 352, 422).

Thus when the Lord Jesus Christ appears in the clouds of heaven, the investigative judgment will have reached its end. "The dead in Christ" will already have been selected, and they will have part in the first resurrection. Likewise chosen are those of the living who will "be caught up together with them in the clouds, to meet the Lord in the air" (1 Thessalonians 4:16, 17). And those left behind will hear the Lord say: "Depart from me, ye that work iniquity" (Matthew 7:23).

At His return Christ will separate the wheat and the tares (Matthew 13:24-30, 36-43). The same conclusion is taught in the parable of the net: "So shall it be at the end of the world: the angels shall come forth, and sever the wicked from among the just" (Matthew 13:49). Then also will be fulfilled the words of Him to whom God "hath given . . . authority to execute judgment also, because he is the Son of man. . . . The hour is coming, in the which all that are in the graves shall hear his voice, and shall come forth; they that have done good, unto the resurrection of life; and they that have done evil, unto the resurrection of damnation" (John 5:27-29).

Christ's return will, therefore, mark the beginning of the second phase of judgment, during which those who have despised God's grace will be judged. "Behold, the Lord cometh with ten thousands of his saints, to execute judgment upon all, and to convince all that are ungodly among them of all their ungodly deeds which they have ungodly committed, and of all their hard speeches which ungodly sinners have spoken against him" (Jude 14, 15). If "judgment must begin at the house of God, . . . what shall the end be of them that obey not the gospel of God? And if the righteous scarcely be saved, where shall the ungodly and the sinner appear?" (1 Peter 4:17, 18).

In this second phase of the judgment, the righteous will serve as members of the jury, we might say. To the Corinthians, who appeared to have forgotten this, Paul gave a reminder: "Do ye not know that the saints shall judge the world? . . . Know ye not that we shall judge angels?" (1 Corinthians 6:2, 3). For God "hath reserved in everlasting chains under darkness unto the judgment of the great day" "the angels which kept not their first estate" (Jude 6).

John saw the redeemed by Christ's side when, during

the millennium, He will judge men and angels who rejected God's appeal. "And I saw thrones, and they sat upon them, and judgment was given unto them: and I saw the souls of them that were beheaded for the witness of Jesus, and for the word of God, and which had not worshipped the beast, neither his image, neither had received his mark upon their foreheads, or in their hands; and they lived and reigned with Christ a thousand years" (Revelation 20:4).

Finally, at the end of the thousand years the third phase of the judgment—the execution of the sentence—will take place. This will be the final act in the great controversy. Once more John described the scene: "And I saw a great white throne, and him that sat on it. . . . And I saw the dead, small and great, stand before God; and the books were opened; and another book was opened, which is the book of life: and the dead were judged out of those things which were written in the books, according to their works" (20:11, 12).

During this majestic scene, "the Son of man shall . . . sit upon the throne of his glory: and before him shall be gathered all nations." Now He will finally "separate them one from another, as a shepherd divideth his sheep from the goats: and he shall set the sheep on his right hand, but the goats on the left. Then shall the King say unto them on his right hand, Come, ye blessed of my Father, inherit the kingdom prepared for you from the foundation of the world. . . . Then shall he say also unto them on the left hand, Depart from me, ye cursed, into everlasting fire, prepared for the devil and his angels" (Matthew 25:31-41).

The separation will not be made by the accident of circumstance or according to a predestination that has foreordained all from eternity. Nobody will be saved or lost without a reason and without knowing why. The Lord takes care to justify His decision. The works of each person have been recorded. The proof is written in the books, and these books are open. Each person will be justified or condemned according to what is written in the books. These books do not necessarily look like those used at the time John wrote the Revelation. Today our methods of recording are much better than those used in the first century, and the ones that the Lord uses are certainly even far superior to ours.

Quite obviously God Himself does not need these books to exercise fair judgment. "Neither is there any creature that is not manifest in his sight: but all things are naked and opened unto the eyes of him with whom we have to do" (Hebrews 4:13). God has no need of conducting a judgment in order to be informed on what we are. Instead He arranges for the different phases of the universal judgment to vindicate Himself, to inform His creatures, and to proclaim His justice and mercy. And when judgment will have been administered, the entire universe will sound forth the song of the Lamb saying: "Great and marvellous are thy works, Lord God Almighty; just and true are thy ways, thou King of saints" (15:3).

That we are judged by our works does not mean, however, that we shall be saved by works. Works are never more than the demonstration of our faith and freedom in Christ. "For by grace are ye saved through faith," but we have been "created in Christ Jesus unto good works, which God hath before ordained that we should walk in them" (Ephesians 2:8, 10).

In the judgment the determining factor on which everything else depends is the attitude of each person toward Christ. Jesus Himself emphasized this. "He that believeth on him is not condemned: but he that believeth not is condemned already, because he hath not believed in the name of the only begotten Son of God. And this is the condemnation, that light is come into the world, and men loved darkness rather than light, because their deeds were evil" (John 3:18, 19).

On another occasion Jesus repeated this truth for the benefit of those who had responded to His appeal. "Verily, verily, I say unto you, He that heareth my word, and believeth on him that sent me, hath everlasting life, and shall not come unto condemnation; but is passed from death unto life" (John 5:24). The apostle Paul expressed the same thing in these words: "There is therefore now no condemnation to them which are in Christ Jesus" (Romans 8:1).

God calls all people, for He has never desired the death

of any sinner but wishes "that he should return from his ways, and live" (Ezekiel 18:23). God has always wanted "all men to be saved, and to come unto the knowledge of the truth" (1 Timothy 2:4). But the response of Jesus' countrymen is typical: "O Jerusalem, Jerusalem, which killest the prophets, and stonest them that are sent unto thee; how often would I have gathered thy children together, as a hen doth gather her brood under her wings, and ye would not!" (Luke 13:34).

The Lord had sent His messengers time after time to call to repentance one generation after another. And what He did in the past, He will do again and again as long as the time of grace remains—especially now in the time of judgment, when each man's destiny is at stake.

The end of our world will not come before the Good News of the kingdom has been preached "in all the world for a witness unto all nations" (Matthew 24:14). At the day and hour fixed for the beginning of the investigative judgment the Lord will work in a spectacular manner so that everyone can hear His last message: "I saw another angel fly in the midst of heaven, having the everlasting gospel to preach unto them that dwell on the earth, and to every nation, and kindred, and tongue, and people, saying with a loud voice, Fear God, and give glory to him; for the hour of his judgment is come" (14:6, 7).

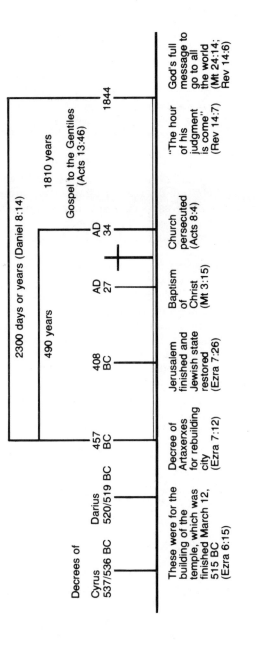

Chapter 9

A Contemporary Message

Whenever there has been an imminent catastrophe, God has raised up messengers or a religious movement to warn men and to call for repentance. For as it is written, "Surely the Lord God will do nothing, but he revealeth his secret unto his servants the prophets" (Amos 3:7).

The Bible is full of these interventions. For the antediluvians the Lord sent Noah to warn them of the Flood, but without success. To Sodom and Gomorrah Lot had the same task, but even his relatives had no desire to believe him. Jonah, in spite of himself, went to Nineveh. And how many other prophets did God raise up? But how were they received? Jesus summed up the reception accorded them as follows: They "beat one, and killed another, and stoned another" (Matthew 21:35). And when the Son of God Himself came, they nailed Him to the cross. "He came unto his own, and his own received him not" (John 1:11). What a sad history of God's efforts for mankind!

How will humanity respond today to God's last appeal before the end of probation? The visions of Revelation do not specify, but God assures us that He will not intervene to "destroy them which destroy the earth" (Revelation 11:18) before having warned all mankind for the last time. John tells us this in the following terms: "I saw another angel fly in the midst of heaven, having the everlasting gospel to preach unto them that dwell on the earth, and to every nation, and kindred, and tongue, and people" (14:6).

The angel with the everlasting gospel along with the two others who follow him with specific messages are clearly symbolic messengers. God has never entrusted the evangelization of the world to angels, but rather to men.

Certainly angels help God's messengers proclaim the gospel, but it falls on us to announce it to the world. As we have already noticed, the word *angel* means "messenger" and often it refers to human messengers as to celestial. The three angels of Revelation 14 stand for all those who in the time of the end receive the everlasting gospel and then proclaim it to "them that dwell on the earth."

"The fact that an angel is said to be the herald of this warning is significant. By the purity, the glory, and the power of the heavenly messenger, divine wisdom has been pleased to represent the exalted character of the work to be accomplished by the message and the power and glory that were to attend it. And the angel's flight 'in the midst of heaven,' the 'loud voice' with which the warning is uttered, and its promulgation to all 'that dwell on the earth'—'to every nation, and kindred, and tongue, and people'—give evidence of the rapidity and world-wide extent of the movement" (*The Great Controversy,* p. 355).

Everything in this prophecy applies to the worldwide work of Adventism, which itself came out of the great religious awakening at the beginning of the nineteenth century. Taking up the interpretation of Daniel's prophecies by their predecessors and in particular by William Miller, the movement was launched with the conviction that on it rested the responsibility to proclaim the threefold message of Revelation 14.

This does not mean that Adventists claim to be the only authentic Christians in the world today or that they alone possess the truth by which men can be saved. But we do have the conviction that God has raised up the Adventist movement at this crucial hour for a specific task. Our task, clearly defined in Revelation 14:6-12, is a worldwide mission: that of proclaiming God's last message "unto them that dwell on the earth, and to every nation, and kindred, and tongue, and people."

Our message is not a new gospel. On the contrary, it is "the everlasting gospel." The apostle Paul took care to say that there was not "another gospel": And even if "an angel from heaven, preach any other gospel unto you than that which we have preached," he wrote, "let him be accursed"

(Galatians 1:6-8). From Genesis to Revelation there is only one and the same gospel. And from the Fall to the restoration of all things the heralds of God have always proclaimed the same Good News, that of the everlasting gospel.

Scripture does not mean that according to time or circumstances one aspect or another of the gospel cannot receive greater emphasis. Depending on its Biblical context, the gospel is described differently also. Thus it is called sometimes "the gospel of God" (Romans 15:16) or "the gospel of Christ" (Galatians 1:7); sometimes the "gospel of the kingdom" (Matthew 24:14) or "the gospel of your salvation" (Ephesians 1:13); sometimes "the gospel of peace" (Ephesians 6:15) or "the gospel of the grace of God" (Acts 20:24).

But whatever the aspect emphasized, the message is truly the gospel only to the extent that it contains all the truths revealed in Scriptures. The gospel is never limited to one aspect alone. For the apostle Paul, "the word of truth" and "the gospel of your salvation" (Ephesians 1:13) were identical, because for him "the gospel" is "the word of the truth" (Colossians 1:5). For him, also, the gospel is recognized by its content: "For other foundation can no man lay than that is laid, which is Jesus Christ" (1 Corinthians 3:11). "Neither is there salvation in any other: for there is none other name under heaven given among men, whereby we must be saved" (Acts 4:12).

To correspond with truth, the preaching of the threefold message of Revelation 14 must necessarily correspond with the everlasting gospel. Furthermore, it must be the everlasting gospel, even when the emphasis is placed on certain special truths. Not supplements to the gospel but rather the everlasting gospel must be presented. First, because it concerns the heavenly courts; then, because of the special preoccupation of contemporary man and his spiritual condition; and finally, because certain fundamental truths of the everlasting gospel have been lost to view or have been totally ignored.

In a certain sense, then, it is possible to say with the apostle Peter that there does exist a "present truth" (2 Peter 1:12), which is nothing more than the everlasting gospel in a contemporary setting. Hence, the threefold message of Revelation 14 is in truth the message for our time. It is good news from God for all those who today love truth and take pleasure in righteousness. In order to understand it better, we will pause for a more detailed study of each message.

The first angel says "with a loud voice, Fear God, and give glory to him; for the hour of his judgment is come: and worship him that made heaven, and earth, and the sea, and the fountains of waters" (14:7). Three imperatives express the conditions for reconciliation with God. In fact, these conditions are the same as those required by God since the creation of the world. They form the foundation itself of the everlasting gospel, and the fact that "the hour of . . . [God's] judgment is come" gives just cause for their urgency.

The fear of God is even more necessary in our time because most individuals in our generation no longer fear God or bother to know Him. Many know "that they which commit such things are worthy of death," but they "not only do the same, but have pleasure in them that do them" (Romans 1:32).

The word *fear* has many different meanings in the Bible, from terror to an expression of love for God. It also expresses equally well the unbelief of men. Certainly, "perfect love casteth out fear" (1 John 4:18), at least that fear which will make sinners tremble in the day of judgment. Yet for the believer it is the beginning of wisdom (Psalm 111:10; Proverbs 1:7)—the expression of his respect and reverence for God. In this vein the Bible declares, "Blessed is the man that feareth the Lord" (Psalm 112:1; compare 128:1), for the mercy of God "is on them that fear him from generation to generation" (Luke 1:50).

Fear thus understood constitutes the way of salvation. "God is no respecter of persons: but in every nation he that feareth him, and worketh righteousness, is accepted with him" (Acts 10:34, 35). It is in the fear of God that the holiness of each believer is perfected (2 Corinthians 7:1) and that the church of Christ is edified (Acts 9:31).

The appeal to fear God is, therefore, perfectly appropriate for our generation, which no longer fears either God or the devil. It indicates, above all, the voice to follow so that we can return to God, because when men who live without hope and without God in the world experience fear toward God, they have made a considerable step already. It is to admit that God exists and thus to show the "beginning of wisdom."

But fear is not all. He wishes further that we give glory to Him. Man was created to be "the image and glory of God" (1 Corinthians 11:7). To give glory to God should be the purpose of all who fear Him. Such was the aim of our Divine Model (John 7:18), to the extent that Jesus could say at the end of His earthly life: "I have glorified thee on the earth: I have finished the work which thou gavest me to do" (John 17:4). Likewise God has "the purchased possession, unto the praise of his glory" (Ephesians 1:14).

God is not satisfied with repentant, converted, pardoned sinners. He wants them to partake of His holiness and to reflect Him more and more, "as in a glass the glory of the Lord" (2 Corinthians 3:18). "Herein is my Father glorified, that ye bear much fruit," said Jesus; "so shall ye be my disciples" (John 15:8). "Let your light so shine before men, that they may see your good works, and glorify your Father which is in heaven" (Matthew 5:16). And "whereas they speak against you as evildoers, they may by your good works, which they shall behold, glorify God in the day of visitation" (1 Peter 2:12).

Finally, to the appeal to fear God and give Him glory the message of the first angel adds the necessity to worship God as the Creator: "Worship him that made heaven, and earth, and the sea, and the fountains of waters" (14:7). From all time men have worshiped false gods, and not even Jesus Himself escaped being faced with this temptation. But we know His firm reaction: "Get thee hence, Satan: for it is written, Thou shalt worship the Lord thy God, and him only shalt thou serve" (Matthew 4:10).

We can adduce several reasons for the first angel's appeal to worship God as the Creator of the universe. First, all that exists is the work of His hands. As the apostle Paul put it so well to the Athenian philosophers: It is He who "made the world and all things therein." It is He, also, who "giveth to all life, and breath, and all things. . . . In him we live, and move, and have our being" (Acts 17:24, 25-28). Creative power is the prerogative of God alone. It distinguishes Him from all false gods (Jeremiah 10:11, 12). For this reason God alone is truly worthy of worship.

Second, what makes the appeal to worship God as Creator especially fitting for our times are the supposedly scientific theories that purely and simply ignore the existence of God. More than anything else the theory of evolution has contributed to the present atheism and has made Christians forget that the God whom they worship is the Creator.

Paul, therefore, was quite correct when he wrote that in the last days there would come a time when men would "not endure sound doctrine; but after their own lusts shall they heap to themselves teachers, having itching ears; and they shall turn away their ears from the truth, and shall be turned unto fables" (2 Timothy 4:3). By rejecting the light of truth, they have become "vain in their imaginations, and their foolish heart was darkened" (Romans 1:21). Because the heart and the spirit are warped, there is no longer any room for the wisdom of the One above. Reasoning can be correct, even showing remarkable intellectual ability. But when the premise does not conform to the truth, all value is taken away from the argument, and inevitably speculative and absurd conclusions are drawn. Having "changed the truth of God into a lie," they have finally "worshipped and served the creature more than the Creator" (Romans 1:25).

Another reason buttresses the call to worship God as Creator—the worship given to the beast and his image, which is dealt with in Revelation 13 and in the third angel's message. Scripture says that "all that dwell upon the earth shall worship him, whose names are not written in the book of life of the Lamb slain" (13:8). Furthermore, is it not added that it would "cause that as many as would not worship the image of the beast should be killed" (13:15)? In the face of this coming religious crisis, the first angel's appeal calls the inhabitants of the earth to choose between the worship of the true God and the false gods of this century, just as the Israelites had to do in the time of the prophet Elijah on Mount Carmel.

Finally, in order that the worship of the true God should be what it ought to be, it must conform to the truth. Jesus explained this to the woman of Samaria: "God is a Spirit: and they that worship him must worship him in spirit and in truth." . . . "For the Father seeketh such to worship him" (John 4:24, 23). The Samaritans certainly worshiped the true God, but without really knowing Him. "Ye worship ye know not what," Jesus said; "we know what we worship: for salvation is of the Jews" (John 4:22). In other words, God asks the worshiper first to know Him in truth and second to abide by the truth.

Worship understood in this way is much more than a question of bowing and praying. Rather it is the acceptance of God's sovereignty and complete submission to His will. The prophet Samuel said this plainly to king Saul who had arrogated to himself the right to worship God in his own way: "Behold, to obey is better than sacrifice, and to hearken than the fat of rams" (1 Samuel 15:22). Jesus expressed the same thought in these words: "Not every one that saith unto me, Lord, Lord, shall enter into the kingdom of heaven; but he that doeth the will of my Father which is in heaven" (Matthew 7:21).

To worship God as Creator, therefore, assumes that worship springs from a respect for the commandment expressly given as a memorial of His creative work: "Remember the sabbath day, to keep it holy: . . . for in six days the Lord made heaven and earth, the sea, and all that in them is, and rested the seventh day: wherefore the Lord blessed the sabbath day, and hallowed it" (Exodus 20:8-11). Furthermore, the Lord desired expressly that the Sabbath should "be a sign . . . that ye may know that I am the Lord your God" (Ezekiel 20:20).

"The importance of the Sabbath as a memorial of creation is that it keeps ever present the true reason why worship is due to God; for the worship of God is based upon the fact that he is the Creator, and that all other beings were created by him. The Sabbath, therefore, lies at the very foundation of divine worship, for it teaches this great truth in the most impressive manner, and no other institution does this. The true ground of divine worship, not of that on the seventh day merely, but of all worship, is found in the distinction between the Creator and his creatures. This great fact can never become obsolete, and must never be forgotten" (J. N. Andrews, *History of the Sabbath*, 3rd edition, p. 515).

"It was to keep this truth ever before the minds of men, that God instituted the Sabbath in Eden; and so long as the fact that He is our Creator continues to be a reason why we should worship Him, so long the Sabbath will continue as its sign and memorial. Had the Sabbath been universally kept, man's thoughts and affections would have been led to the Creator as the object of reverence and worship, and there would never have been an idolater, an atheist, or an infidel. The keeping of the Sabbath is a sign of loyalty to the true God, 'Him that made heaven, and earth, and the sea, and the fountains of waters.' It follows that the message which commands men to worship God and keep His commandments will especially call upon them to keep the fourth commandment" (*The Great Controversy*, p. 438).

In "the hour of temptation, which shall come upon all the world, to try them that dwell upon the earth" (3:10), the question of the day of rest will be the touchstone of each person's faithfulness. First, because it is the sign by which the believer recognizes God as the Creator and shows his obedience to His holy commandments; then, because the question of the day of rest will be the point of truth particularly controverted.

The promise of God's protection is for those who will have learned to keep "the word of . . . [His] patience" in response to the first angel's appeal to fear God, to give Him glory, and to worship Him in spirit and in truth. In a time such as ours it is certainly the message that the world needs. May it be heard by "them that dwell on the earth, . . . every nation, and kindred, and tongue, and people"!

Chapter 10

Come Out of Babylon

The second angel's message reveals a new aspect of the everlasting gospel. At first sight it seems to be a simple statement of an incurable situation. Yet when we consider it in the light of the complementary message in chapter 18, proclaimed at the end of probation, we can see that it is a supreme appeal of divine mercy.

By exposing the real situation of the world in the time of the end, God hopes to stir the conscience of all who are still open to hear His messages. In addition to the words: "Babylon is fallen, is fallen, that great city, because she made all nations drink of the wine of the wrath of her fornication" (14:8; compare 18:2), the Lord invites: "Come out of her, my people, that ye be not partakers of her sins, and that ye receive not of her plagues" (18:4).

Clearly the content of the second angel's message is symbolic, but considered in the Biblical context in general, and in that of the Revelation in particular, anyone can easily fathom its mystery.

At the outset we should resolve a minor time problem. It is written that the second angel "followed" the first. The Greek word used here can be equally well translated by the verbs *follow* or *accompany*. The text probably suggests both meanings. From the point of view of time the second angel follows the first. But from the aspect of duration the first angel continues giving his message while the second angel's message "accompanies" it. Historically in the Adventist Church they follow in order. The Millerite preachers presented the second angel's message for the first time during the summer of 1844 and applied it to the churches that had rejected the first angel's message on judgment. But until the end of probation, the two messages will go together and should be preached simultaneously.

The meaning of the second angel's message depends entirely on our understanding of the expression "Babylon the great," repeated in its various forms six times in the Revelation (14:8; 16:19; 17:5; 18:2, 10, 21). The number six, moreover, is part of the mystery of Babylon. It is to Babylonian worship what the number seven is in the Bible. Because "Babylon the great" is a "mystery" (17:5), it can only be understood by the help of revelation.

The expression cannot refer to the ancient city of Babylon, for it lay in ruins when John wrote these words. Babylon here symbolizes a mysterious reality that must be defined first with the help of the history of this city and then with the aid of the context in the Revelation.

The city of Babylon, founded by Nimrod (Genesis 10:9, 10), was the center of the first great apostasy of history, during the construction of the tower of Babel (Genesis 11:1-9). Babylon reached the height of its glory and power under the reign of Nebuchadnezzar in the time of the prophet Daniel. Nebuchadnezzar's pride in Babylon—"Is not this great Babylon, that I have built for the house of the kingdom by the might of my power, and for the honour of my majesty?" (Daniel 4:30)—finds a certain echo in our text in the Revelation.

Because Babylon destroyed Jerusalem and the temple and then carried God's people into exile, its name came to denote the enemy of God's people and of the truth. Both Jews and Christians have thus used the word *Babylon* of Rome, which persecuted them. The apostle Peter, following this example in his first epistle, wrote to the Christians in Asia Minor from "the church that is at Babylon, elected together with you" (1 Peter 5:13). The church fathers, such as Irenaeus and Tertullian, do the same when speaking of Rome or of the Roman Empire.

Clearly, then, "Babylon the great" as used in the Revelation crystallizes all this name signified at that time for God's people. The adjective *great,* which Babylon prided itself on, perfectly fits a power that dominated the world and was hostile to the worship of the true God. Its greatness in the

Revelation is above all a measure of negative values. Great is its moral fall, "for her sins have reached unto heaven, and God hath remembered her iniquities" (18:5).

It is interesting to note that in the Old Testament as in the New, Babylon is constantly in opposition to Jerusalem. While Babylon symbolized pride and human glory as well as self-adoration, Jerusalem represented the honor and glory of God, as well as the worship of the only true God. Babylon indicated rebellion against God, apostasy, and confusion, but Jerusalem meant peace, faithfulness, and unity. The Revelation likens Babylon to a "great whore" (17:1), but it describes Jerusalem "as a bride adorned for her husband" (21:2).

By this last comparison the Revelation rightly provides an additional element of identification. "Babylon the great" is here personified as a woman. As we have already explained, in prophecy a woman always symbolizes God's people, whether they be Israel in the Old Testament or the Christian church in the New Testament. When this symbolic woman is unfaithful to her Divine Husband, she is called an adulteress or a harlot.

In fact, Revelation calls "Babylon the great" "the great whore" (17:1). And the prophet describes her as such. "Arrayed in purple and scarlet colour, and decked with gold and precious stones and pearls," she holds "a golden cup in her hand full of abominations and filthiness of her fornication" (17:4). In addition, the "many waters" on which "the whore sitteth," the angel explains to the prophet, "are peoples, and multitudes, and nations, and tongues" (17:15).

That "the kings of the earth have committed fornication" with her (17:2) shows clearly what kind of prostitution is meant: a union of church and state. And when the woman sits upon the beast (17:3), this means that the church dominates the state and that she reigns as a mistress to accomplish her ends. Because history illustrates what happens each time such a situation arises, we can understand the prophet's amazement when he "saw the woman drunken with the blood of the saints, and with the blood of the martyrs of Jesus" (17:6).

It was not necessary, however, to wait until the nineteenth century before someone recognized that this description refers to the Christian church in its union with the Roman Empire. Joachim of Floris, celebrated for his interpretation of prophecy, during the twelfth century saw in the mystic Babylon of Revelation the church of his own time. Toward the end of the Middle Ages several other Christian leaders thought the same, including John Huss and Savonarola. With the Reformers this identification became current in Protestantism.

It is not surprising, then, that William Miller adopted the same interpretation when he began preaching the second angel's message in 1844. But as a matter of fact, Miller included in Babylon the Protestant churches that had rejected the message of Christ's soon return.

The pioneers of the Adventist movement followed this interpretation. Joseph Bates wrote: "*Mystery Babylon . . .* represents the organized Churches of all descriptions, divided into three parts, Rev. XVI, 19, viz: Roman, Greek, and Protestant. . . .

"Our business then is with the Protestant Church, for it will be admitted by all that the Roman and Greek church[es] are corrupt and anti-Christian" (*The Advent Review*, November, 1850, p. 67).

In a less specific manner James White wrote: "The woman, which is the great city, called Babylon, symbolizes the fallen apostate churches" (*The Review and Herald*, August 5, 1851, p. 3).

J. N. Andrews said that Babylon included "all the corrupt religious bodies which ever have existed, or which exist at the present time, united to the world, and sustained by the civil power," including "the corrupt Jewish Church," "the corrupt Papal and Greek churches," and "the great body of the Protestant churches" that "imitate the Romish church" (*The Review and Herald*, February 21, 1854, p. 36). Uriah Smith in *Daniel and the Revelation* took up this interpretation, and Ellen G. White in *The Great Controversy* did the same.

"SDA interpretation today is essentially that of Uriah Smith and other early SDA commentators. Modern Babylon is understood to stand for all Christian churches that have departed from the 'everlasting gospel' as set forth in the Scriptures, including both the great Roman apostasy of the early Christian centuries and the more recent departure of Protestantism from God's Word, beginning in particular with their rejection of the 1844 message. The fall is understood to be progressive; it is not yet complete, but it will be so when the major Protestant churches collaborate with the Church of Rome in an attempt to coerce the conscience (Revelation 13). The second angel's message of Revelation 14:8 is a warning that Babylon has fallen, and chapter 18:1-4 is a call to God's people to come out of Babylon, in order to avoid complicity in her crimes and a share in her 'plagues' " (*Seventh-day Adventist Encyclopedia*, revised edition, p. 115).

Now it is not difficult to understand what the second angel's message means by the expression "Babylon is fallen." This declaration echoes a prophetic passage of the Old Testament: "Babylon is fallen, is fallen; and all the graven images of her gods he hath broken unto the ground" (Isaiah 21:9). Since mystic Babylon represents all the churches and religious movements who are unfaithful to the eternal gospel, the fall is primarily spiritual.

Luther was right in writing: "Wherever you see that there is no gospel (as we see in the synagogue of the papists and the Thomists) there must be no doubt that there is no longer the church there" (*Ad. librum . . . Ambrosis Catharini*, W. A. 7, 721, 4). Calvin agreed: "If the foundation of the church is the doctrine of the apostles and the prophets, . . . if this doctrine is removed, how can the building remain standing?" (J. de Senarclens, *De la Vraie Eglise selon Calvin*, p. 17).

When the church succumbed to the thinking of the time, the very foundations of the church were undermined, and the building was ready to collapse. For some centuries the church had been crumbling under the weight of all the teachings contrary to the Bible, such as the immortality of the soul, the eternal punishment of the wicked, and the sacredness of the first day of the week in place of the Sabbath. But when theologians themselves turned away from the authenticity of the Bible, from the divinity of Jesus Christ, and from the veracity of all the miracles, the consequences were incurable.

Notice the observation of Professor Randall from Columbia University on the subject of the Christian heritage: "Today it seems that the great Hebrew-Christian moral tradition, the most ancient part of our heritage, is crumbling to pieces before our very eyes. . . . The man who trusts a physical science to describe the world finds no conceivable place into which to fit a deity" (cited by Roy Allan Anderson, *Unfolding the Revelation,* p. 153).

As to the Christian hope of Christ's return, James Gilkey summed up the opinion of contemporary religious leaders thus: "Today the ancient belief that Jesus will reappear in the sky, inaugurate a dramatic world judgment, . . . has dwindled from a universally accepted and enormously influential Christian conviction to the esoteric doctrine of a minority. Once a modern man accepts what historians tell him about the age of the universe, and once he accepts what scientists tell him about the nature of the evolutionary process, he cannot believe that there will ever be any such spectacular wind-up of the world's affairs as the one which the early Christians believed would presently take place" (*ibid.,* p. 154).

Such views form a clear witness that "Babylon the great" has really fallen, and it would be easy to paint a gloomy picture of so-called Christian society, which, to be truthful, is Christian in name only. But we shall content ourselves with the revealing description of the prophetic word: "Babylon . . . is become the habitation of devils, and the hold of every foul spirit, and a cage of every unclean and hateful bird. For all nations have drunk of the wine of the wrath of her fornication, and the kings of the earth have committed fornication with her, and the merchants of the earth are waxed rich through the abundance of her delicacies" (18:2, 3).

Spiritual Babylon conforms to the detailed analysis made by the apostle Paul concerning the decadence of those "who hold the truth in unrighteousness" (Romans 1:18). God gives "them up to uncleanness through the lusts of their own hearts," "unto vile affections," "to a reprobate mind, to do those things which are not convenient" (verses 24, 26, 28). Although they know "the judgment of God, that they which commit such things are worthy of death," they "not only do the same, but have pleasure in them that do them" (verse 32).

Commenting on this passage Ellen G. White writes: "A terrible picture of the condition of the world has been presented before me. Immorality abounds everywhere. Licentiousness is the special sin of this age. Never did vice lift its deformed head with such boldness as now. The people seem to be benumbed, and the lovers of virtue and true goodness are nearly discouraged by its boldness, strength, and prevalence.

"I was referred to Romans 1:18-32, as a true description of the world previous to the second appearing of Christ" (Ellen G. White, *Child Guidance*, p. 440).

Such conditions would make us lose all hope had not God assured us that once more He will make light shine in the intense darkness of the time of the end. Here is what the prophetic word says at the end of its description of the work of Babylon. "After these things I saw another angel come down from heaven, having great power; and the earth was lightened with his glory. And he cried mightily with a strong voice, saying, Babylon the great is fallen, is fallen. . . . And I heard another voice from heaven, saying, Come out of her, my people, that ye be not partakers of her sins, and that ye receive not of her plagues" (18:1-4).

Even though Babylon is fallen, there is still a multitude of genuine believers scattered in its midst. Many probably have not yet heard the Good News. Some have not completely understood the teaching of Christ. Others are still waiting to see clearly the signs of apostasy in the churches they attend. Many Christians suffer when they see their spiritual leaders abandon the sound doctrine of God's Word. The day is coming when all those who love the truth and "them also that love his appearing" (2 Timothy 4:8) will perfectly understand the second angel's message and will respond to God's invitation to come out of Babylon.

"We are living in the last days of this earth's history, in

an age of sin and corruption, and like Noah we are to so live that we shall be a pleasure to God, showing forth the praises of Him 'who hath called you out of darkness into his marvelous light' (1 Peter 2:9). In the prayer which Christ offered to His Father just before His crucifixion, He said, 'I pray not that thou shouldest take them out of the world, but that thou shouldest keep them from the evil' (John 17:15)" (*Selected Messages*, Book One, p. 90).

Chapter 11

A Solemn Warning

The first angel's message calls "them that dwell on the earth, and . . . every nation, and kindred, and tongue, and people" to "fear God, and give glory to him: . . . and worship him," "for the hour of his judgment is come." The second angel's message condemns all worship that does not harmonize with the everlasting gospel. God invites His children who are still scattered in Babylon to come out of apostate Christianity so they will not partake of her sins and participate in her plagues.

To the third angel is entrusted the task of warning mankind of the tragic consequences that arise quite naturally from indifference to the Lord's merciful appeals. This message contains the most terrible warning God has ever given to men. Since it is of utmost importance, the angel proclaims it "with a loud voice" (14:9), for the whole world must hear it.

"If any man worship the beast and his image, and receive his mark in his forehead, or in his hand, the same shall drink of the wine of the wrath of God, which is poured out without mixture into the cup of his indignation; and he shall be tormented with fire and brimstone in the presence of the holy angels, and in the presence of the Lamb: and the smoke of their torment ascendeth up for ever and ever: and they have no rest day nor night, who worship the beast and his image, and whosoever receiveth the mark of his name.

"Here is the patience of the saints: here are they that keep the commandments of God, and the faith of Jesus.

"And I heard a voice from heaven saying unto me, Write, Blessed are the dead which die in the Lord from henceforth: Yea, saith the Spirit, that they may rest from their labours; and their works do follow them" (14:9-13).

Because of the importance of this message and the wealth of its content, we shall study it in two separate chapters. In any case, the message itself comes to us in two clearly distinct parts. The first is directed to those who worship the beast and his image. It warns them of the terrible consequences in store for them if they continue to despise the appeals of divine mercy (14:9-11). The second part, on the other hand, deals with those who will have endured unto the end in obedience and whom the Lord rewards with everlasting happiness (14:12, 13).

On the whole, the third angel's message defines true worship in contrast to that which is only a counterfeit. Likewise it portrays the inevitable consequences resulting from both—either eternal life or eternal death. There is no in-between choice. This message also confronts each person with a choice on which his eternal destiny ultimately depends. For this reason, too, the message must be heard by everybody, so that everyone can decide in full knowledge of the issues.

The first part of the message is expressed in complicated language, but if it had been expressed other than by symbols, it would never have reached us. The powers concerned would have taken care to make it disappear. Presented in this way, the message remains a mystery for all who do not understand the Scriptures. Jesus' reason for speaking in parables also applies here: "Therefore speak I to them in parables: because they seeing see not; and hearing they hear not, neither do they understand" (Matthew 13:13).

The issue at stake is very simple: God warns against the worship of the powers of this age, which are personified by "the beast and his image," whose "mark" of authority is placed in the forehead or in the hand of its worshipers. The difficulty lies in the identification of these powers. However the symbols used are not new. Revelation 13 is devoted to them entirely. It is indispensable, therefore, to refer to this chapter so that we can understand what they stand for. We shall consider first "the beast," then "the image of the beast," and finally "the mark of his name."

The description of the beast in Revelation 13 comes from the prophecy found in Daniel 7. A simple comparison between these two chapters allows us to recognize in the beast with two horns the Roman Empire. Revelation 13 describes it as a combination of the empires that preceded it—namely, the Greco-Macedonian leopard, the Medo-Persian bear, and the Babylonian lion. In both instances the prophecy describes the appearance of a power that arises from the heart of the Roman Empire after its division into ten parts. It refers to none other than the Papacy. The time of its appearance, the characteristic details, the period of its activity, all lead to this conclusion.

One need not be a historian to know that the Roman emperors gave their power to the bishops of Rome. Revelation expresses it in these words: "The dragon gave him his power, and his seat, and great authority" (13:2). The Papacy exercised this authority for forty-two prophetic months (13:5), that is, for 1260 years, the same time period mentioned also in Daniel 7:25. The historical application covers the period of papal supremacy from AD 538 to 1798. The two prophetic books also mention the same methods used to subdue the rebels and heretics: seduction, political pressure, persecution, and war against the saints. The objective is clearly indicated several times: to make "all that dwell upon the earth" to worship the beast (13:4-8).

So far there is nothing really new in Revelation 13. God had already revealed all these details to the prophet Daniel. One can only be struck by the resemblance, which is not limited to the symbols but which corresponds word for word in the expressions used. This repetition was indispensable so that the reader could locate the really new details in the prophecy. These new details in Revelation 13:3 indicate that the power in question would receive a "deadly wound" but that its deadly wound would be healed.

We have already mentioned that this deadly wound was inflicted on the Papacy in 1798, when Pope Pius VI was taken prisoner and led into exile. The prophecy could not have stated the event more clearly: "He that leadeth into captivity shall go into captivity: he that killeth with the sword must be killed with the sword" (13:10). But who could have predicted a renewal of papal power as does the prophecy of Revelation when it specifies that the "deadly wound" would be healed and that "all the world . . . [would wonder] after the beast" (13:3)?

This particular detail is itself the subject of the second part of the thirteenth chapter; which refers to "the image of the beast." John saw a second beast appear, which "causeth the earth and them which dwell therein to worship the first beast, whose deadly wound was healed" (13:12). "By the means of those miracles which he had power to do," he deceives the whole world and says "to them that dwell on the earth, that they should make an image to the beast, which had the wound by a sword, and did live" (13:13, 14). In other words, the prophecy predicts a replica or "image" of the politico-religious power such as it was before the deadly wound.

The prophecy further specifies that "he had power to give life unto the image of the beast, that the image of the beast should both speak, and cause that as many as would not worship the image of the beast should be killed" (13:15). This means that the plan of a politico-religious power in the image of the Papacy would succeed. It would begin to promulgate laws, going as far as to punish with death those who would not sumit to its authority. In short it would behave just as did the little horn of Daniel 7, "that spake very great things" and that oppressed "the saints of the most High" (Daniel 7:20, 25). Revelation words it this way: He "opened his mouth in blasphemy against God, to blaspheme his name" and to "war with the saints" (13:6, 7).

So, the "beast" and "the image of the beast," which are the subjects of the third angel's message, are thus identified. Now we need to find the meaning of "the mark of his name." In the final crisis this mark will serve as a distinctive sign of the worshipers "of the image of the beast." "And he causeth all, both small and great, rich and poor, free and bond, to receive a mark in their right hand, or in their foreheads: and that no man might buy or sell, save he that had the mark, or the name of the beast, or the number of his name" (13:16, 17). What, then, is this mark?

Clearly it is a distinguishing mark that serves as a kind of seal or symbol of the power concerned. For the one who receives it, it signifies his submission to the authority so represented. That it is received in the right hand or in the forehead shows that the mark has to do with the work or the religion of the recipient. The Passover served a similar function for ancient Israel: "And it shall be for a sign unto thee upon thine hand, and for a memorial between thine eyes" (Exodus 13:9). Adventists see in this mark a day of worship.

Numerous commentators have shown that the institution of Sunday as a day of worship corresponds to this criterion. In fact, Sunday is not only the official day of weekly rest, but it is also the visible sign of the religious convictions of those who keep it. It is, furthermore, the outstanding sign of papal authority. Over the years Catholic theologians have insisted that the institution of Sunday signified the authority of the church. In his arguments with the Lutherans, Johann Eck underlined the inconsistency of the Reformation church, which continued to observe Sunday, despite the testimony of Scripture.

"Sunday . . . is purely a creation of the Catholic Church."

"For ages all Christian nations looked to the Catholic Church, and, as we have seen, the various states enforced by law her ordinances as to worship and cessation of labor on Sunday. Protestantism, in discarding the authority of the Church, has no good reason for its Sunday theory, and ought, logically, to keep Saturday as the Sabbath" (John Gilmary Shea, "The Observance of Sunday and Civil Laws for Its Enforcement," *The American Catholic Quarterly Review*, January, 1883, pp. 139, 152).

This sign of authority that the Catholic Church so readily claims for itself constitutes an additional proof of the fulfillment of the prophecy we are now studying. Among the deeds of the Papacy mentioned by Daniel is that it would "think to change times and laws" (Daniel 7:25). Now in the law of God only the fourth commandment relates to time. God gave the Sabbath as the memorial of creation, and consequently it constitutes the sign that distinguishes the worshipers of the true God (Ezekiel 20:20), just as Sunday is the distinguishing mark of the worshipers of "the beast and his image."

During the final conflict described in the prophecy of Revelation 13, just as in the third angel's message, Sunday and the Sabbath will distinguish the two classes of worshipers. This conflict, it must be said, has not yet begun. It will come only at the time indicated by prophecy—after the healing of the beast's "deadly wound" (13:3) and after "the image of the beast" will have been set up (13:15). Only then will Sunday become "the mark," without which it will be impossible to "buy or sell," in other words, to live.

"There are now true Christians in every church, not excepting the Roman Catholic communion, who honestly believe that Sunday is the Sabbath of divine appointment. God accepts their sincerity of purpose and their integrity before Him. But when Sunday observance shall be enforced by law, and the world shall be enlightened concerning the obligation of the true Sabbath, then whoever shall transgress the command of God, to obey a precept which has no higher authority than that of Rome, will thereby honor popery above God. He is paying homage to Rome and to the power which enforces the institution ordained by Rome. He is worshiping the beast and his image. As men then reject the institution which God has declared to be the sign of His authority, and honor in its stead that which Rome has chosen as the token of her supremacy, they will thereby accept the sign of allegiance to Rome—'the mark of the beast.' And it is not until the issue is thus plainly set before the people, and they are brought to choose between the commandments of God and the commandments of men, that those who continue in transgression will receive 'the mark of the beast' " (*The Great Controversy*, p. 449).

Nothing has been said thus far about "another beast [that] . . . had two horns like a lamb," which John saw "coming up out of the earth" (13:11). It is by his intervention that "the image of the beast" will be created—this politico-religious institution in which the church will dominate the state in order to sustain its dogmas. In the late 1600s Thomas Goodwin, vice chancellor of Oxford University, advanced the idea that this could refer to a state Protestantism of which England was then an example.

However, as John Wesley very well remarked, in 1755, "But he is not yet come, though he cannot be far off; for he is to appear at the end of the forty-two months of the first beast" (*Explanatory Notes Upon the New Testament*, p. 1010). Recognizing the certainty of this chronological detail, numerous commentators of the first half of the nineteenth century held, then, that Revelation 13 referred to a Protestant power of the future whose two characteristics would be civil and religious liberty as symbolized by the "two horns like a lamb" (13:11).

John N. Andrews in *The Review and Herald*, May 19, 1851, identified the United States of America as being the Protestant power symbolized in this prophecy. Three months later Joseph Bates endeavored to prove that only the United States of America could fit the facts of Revelation 13:11 (*The Review and Herald*, August 5, 1851). Finally in his *Review and Herald* of August 19, 1851, James White confirmed this point of view. But it was not without emotion that he wrote: "The rise of our own nation, with its two leading principles, Protestantism and Republicanism, answers the prophetic description of the beast 'coming up out of the earth' having 'two horns like a lamb' " (p. 12). From then on, this interpretation became that of the heralds of the threefold message of Revelation 14.

Ellen G. White approved of this understanding when she wrote: "The application of the symbol admits of no question. One nation, and only one, meets the specifications of this prophecy; it points unmistakably to the United States of America" (*The Great Controversy*, p. 440).

What should we think, then, of the prophecy that the United States would one day speak "as a dragon"? At first sight this would appear fanciful, but when we look at it more closely, numerous signs enable us to foresee the change spoken of by the prophecy. "In order for the United States to form an image of the beast, the religious power must so control the civil government that the authority of the state will also be employed by the church to accomplish her own ends.

"Whenever the church has obtained secular power, she has employed it to punish dissent from her doctrines. Protestant churches that have followed in the steps of Rome by forming alliance with worldly powers have manifested a similar desire to restrict liberty of conscience."

"When the leading churches of the United States, uniting upon such points of doctrine as are held by them in common, shall influence the state to enforce their decrees and to sustain their institutions, then Protestant America will have formed an image of the Roman hierarchy, and the infliction of civil penalties upon dissenters will inevitably result" (*ibid.*, pp. 443, 445).

It is important to notice that this interpretation of the prophecy originated before the political and religious events that confirm it more and more in our day. Besides, have we not reached the time for the healing of the Papacy's deadly wound, which occurs just before the starting point for the working of the power destined to "make an image to the beast" (13:14)? It is even surprising to note that the restoration of papal power coincides with the elevation of the United States as a leader of world politics. Furthermore, since the last world war there has been a systematic agreement over the world politics of the Vatican and of the United States.

Already in 1948 Frédéric Hoffet had deplored this fact in his book *Protestant Imperialism.* "American politics itself has in this indirect way suffered by the influence of the Roman church, . . . which has succeeded thus in tarnishing the image of the great Protestant republic before the world."

"There is something tragic to see the descendants of the Pilgrim Fathers today support a Franco and perhaps other candidates for dictatorship also, who will stifle liberty once they gain power. What if, urged by fear of Communism, America, blinded, would however give in to the solicitations of Rome that she should be on her guard: she would be unfaithful to herself. Allied to a church which has always stood for, if not absolutism, at least intolerance, she would lose immediately, with this moral radiance which makes all those who do not wish to abandon their ideal of liberty look towards her, the right of defending throughout the world the great principles on which she has erected her democracy" (pp. 234, 244).

Alas! these thoughts are only too true today. With giant strides the world marches in the direction foretold by prophecy. Also the three angels' messages have never been more apt than in our day. It behooves all who know them to proclaim them in all the world with all the power of their voices. Every inhabitant of the earth must hear the call of the everlasting gospel. Everybody should know that there is no more to hope for in this present world. All should be invited to take their stand, knowing the full consequences and having understood the gravity of what is at stake. For if eternal life is promised to those who shall endure to the end by the obedience of faith, eternal death is the fate of those who will not have believed the truth. Those who have taken pleasure in drinking "the wine of the wrath of . . . [the] fornication" of Babylon the great will also "drink of the wine of the wrath of God, which is poured out without mixture into the cup of his indignation" (14:8, 10).

Chapter 12

The Message of
Justification by Faith

In His prophetic discourse Jesus described the general attitude of mankind in the last days and its effect on His disciples: "And because iniquity shall abound, the love of many shall wax cold" (Matthew 24:12). In other words, the majority of Christians have become worldly because of a growing and systematic rejection of God's commandments, for actually the Greek word translated "iniquity" literally means "lawlessness."

However, Jesus does not dwell on this dramatic statement. He wishes above all to emphasize once more the only way of salvation. So He adds immediately: "But he that shall endure unto the end, the same shall be saved" (verse 13). Now the third angel's message specifies what endurance means: "Here is the patience ["endurance," RSV] of the saints: here are they that keep the commandments of God, and the faith of Jesus" (14:12).

In his epistles the apostle Paul also speaks of these same two factors. He calls the first "the mystery of iniquity" (2 Thessalonians 2:7), which he saw already at work in the Apostolic Church and which would grow until the Lord's coming. Due to Satan's mysterious work, Paul explained, men would submit to the influence of a "strong delusion, that they should believe a lie: that they all might be damned who believed not the truth, but had pleasure in unrighteousness" (verses 11, 12).

But Paul also spoke of the "mystery of godliness," which he described as "great." According to him, Christ "was manifest in the flesh, justified in the Spirit, seen of angels, preached unto the Gentiles, believed on in the world, received up into glory" (1 Timothy 3:16). This mystery is nothing less than God's plan, realized in Jesus Christ, for the salvation of mankind.

The two mysteries also form the content of the third angel's message. The mystery of iniquity in the time of the end will climax in the insidious work of the beast and his image. The coming wicked one will reveal the methods of Satan "with all power and signs and lying wonders, and with all deceivableness of unrighteousness." But, "the Lord shall consume [him] with the spirit of his mouth, and shall destroy [him] with the brightness of his coming" (2 Thessalonians 2:9, 10, 8). These verses describe the content of the first part of the third angel's message, which the previous chapter dealt with.

Now we will dwell on the second part of this message, which relates to "the mystery of godliness." This part shows the different aspects in which the Good News of salvation should be understood and preached in our time. For as a result of the amoral and immoral attitude of a large number of our contemporaries, many today are confused over this vital point.

After centuries of belief in salvation by works apart from faith, the Reformers revived Paul's teaching that salvation is by grace, by faith, and without works. Following which the Protestant churches, generally speaking, concluded that the gospel had freed Christians from the requirements of the law. Many came to believe that Christ's life and death exempted the Christian from the necessity of living in harmony with God's commandments. "The desire for an easy religion that requires no striving, no self-denial, no divorce from the follies of the world, has made the doctrine of faith, and faith only, a popular doctrine" (*The Great Controversy*, p. 472).

This understanding of justification by faith has led Christianity to a conclusion opposite to what Jesus and the apostles really taught. Many Christians readily think today that Christianity has softened the religion of the Old Testament. Most frequently they contrast Christianity with Judaism—a religion of love and forgiveness in contradistinction to a religion of severity and justice. They even go so far as to set the God of the gospel against the God of Israel.

Emphasizing still more this contrast, the Protestant churches in particular speak of Jewish law and Christian grace, concluding that the reign of grace has permanently superseded the reign of the law.

Such interpretations are, in actual fact, at the root of the dissolute so-called Christian society of today. One need not look any further for an explanation of the anarchy rampant in the world. However, nothing is more removed from the teaching of the everlasting gospel. This interpretation concludes that man's liberty—and hence his salvation—is found in freedom from all law, divine or human. But against this ideology, which in its most virulent form proclaims man's complete autonomy, the third angel's message of Revelation 14 urges faithfulness to "the commandments of God" and encourages keeping "the faith of Jesus."

This message, then, brings to a head what justification by faith really means. Opposing the error of relying on one's own works to gain God's favor, it recalls simply that "a man is justified by faith without the deeds of the law" (Romans 3:28). "Not by works of righteousness which we have done, but according to his mercy he saved us; . . . that being justified by his grace, we should be made heirs according to the hope of eternal life" (Titus 3:5-7).

"He who is trying to become holy by his own works in keeping the law, is attempting an impossibility. All that man can do without Christ is polluted with selfishness and sin. It is the grace of Christ alone, through faith, that can make us holy" (Ellen G. White, *Steps to Christ,* p. 60).

Against "the opposite and no less dangerous error . . . that belief in Christ releases men from keeping the law of God" (*ibid.*) the third angel's message invites Christians to "keep the commandments of God." For as the apostle Paul wrote, love is not against the requirements of the law; on the contrary, "love is the fulfilling of the law" (Romans 13:10). Or as the apostle John said: "This is the love of God that we keep his commandments" (1 John 5:3). So "he that saith, I know him, and keepeth not his commandments, is a liar, and the truth is not in him" (1 John 2:4). For in essence, "not the hearers of the law are just before God, but the doers of the law shall be justified" (Romans 2:13). And to those inclined to forget, Paul declared even further that the keeping of the commandments of God is everything (1 Corinthians 7:19).

This is why the third angel's message emphasizes that the patience of the saints is characterized by the keeping of "the commandments of God, and the faith of Jesus." There is no genuine Christian life otherwise. It is not a matter of choosing between faith or works, between law or grace. It is never one or the other, but always one and the other. Works are the fruits of faith. Obedience to the law is the effect of grace. According to the everlasting gospel there is no opposition between faith and works or between law and grace. On the contrary, they are complementary.

"As the body without the spirit is dead, so faith without works is dead also" (James 2:26). Faith exists only to the extent that it produces works. For this reason James can say again that "faith without works is dead" and "that by works a man is justified, and not by faith only" (verses 20, 24).

Nor did the apostle Paul teach differently. Not only did he affirm forcibly that we are not saved *by* works, but he also declared with no less vigor that we are saved *unto* good works. "We are his workmanship, created in Christ Jesus *unto* good works, which God hath before ordained that we should walk in them" (Ephesians 2:10). A wild tree is not grafted *because* it bears good fruit but *in order that* it will bear good fruit afterward. And just as a tree is known by its fruit, so faith is recognized by its works. "Do we then make void the law through faith?" asked Paul. "God forbid," he replied. "Yea, we establish the law" (Romans 3:31).

"That so-called faith in Christ which professes to release men from the obligation of obedience to God, is not faith, but presumption" (*ibid.*, p. 61). "Instead of releasing man from obedience, it is faith, and faith only, that makes us partakers of the grace of Christ, which enables us to render obedience" (*ibid.*, pp. 60, 61). It is in this sense that Luke spoke of the "great company of the priests [who] were obedient to the faith" (Acts 6:7). Similarly Paul wrote that he had "received grace and apostleship" from Jesus Christ "for obedience to the faith among all nations, for his name"

(Romans 1:5). This is also why he wished to make the gospel of salvation "known to all nations for the obedience of faith" (Romans 16:26).

No one has defined the indispensable role of the law in the process of salvation by grace better than the apostle Paul. Without the law, faith and grace would be useless. In fact, it is by the law that we have knowledge of sin. Paul wrote, "I had not known sin, but by the law" (Romans 7:7). It is the mirror by which everyone can see himself as he is. Without it there is no sense of sin whatever, and consequently, no need of a Saviour, and furthermore, no need of grace. But along with a sense of guilt the law also creates in man the desire to be delivered from guilt. And so in this way the law acts as a "schoolmaster to bring us unto Christ, that we might be justified by faith" (Galatians 3:24; compare Romans 3:24 and Ephesians 2:8).

But according to the writers of both the Old and the New Testaments, the law has still another function: that of making known the will of God. Being the expression of God's thought and character, the law is consequently the expression of His justice, perfection, and love. Paul declared: "Wherefore the law is holy, and the commandment holy, and just, and good" (Romans 7:12). It contains the moral principles that man needs so he can distinguish between good and evil and can live in harmony with God and his fellowman.

The failure of the law to assure us of eternal life springs from the sinful nature of man. "The law is spiritual: but I am carnal, sold under sin" (verse 14). "The carnal mind is enmity against God: for it is not subject to the law of God, neither indeed can be" (Romans 8:7).

Yet by our faith in Jesus Christ God does not free us from obedience to His commandments, but rather He frees us from sin and enables us to do His will. "God sending his own Son in the likeness of sinful flesh, and for sin, condemned sin in the flesh: that the righteousness of the law might be fulfilled in us" (verses 3, 4). That is why "being . . . made free from sin," we have become "servants of righteousness," for we are always slaves to the one we obey, "whether of sin unto death, or of obedience unto righteousness" (Romans 6:18, 16).

Thus the law leads the sinner to Christ, and Christ brings back the repentant, forgiven, and regenerated sinner to the law. Far, then, from abrogating the law, the new convenant confirms it. What is changed is the relationship between man and the law. No longer will the law be simply external to man, graven "in tables of stone" (2 Corinthians 3:3), but God says: "I will put my laws into their mind, and write them in their hearts" (Hebrews 8:10).

The work of grace, therefore, establishes God's law in the heart of him who accepts Jesus Christ by faith as Lord and Saviour from then on, having been released from a purely legal obedience to the letter of the law, which kills, the Christian is made capable of obeying the commandment in the spirit, which gives life (2 Corinthians 3:6). The grace of God produces in him "obedience of faith," or "an obedient faith."

To the rich young ruler who wanted to know how he could inherit eternal life, Jesus replied very simply: "If thou wilt enter into life, keep the commandments" (Matthew 19:17). "Which?" the young man asked. And Jesus referred him to the Ten Commandments. Of them Jesus said: "Till heaven and earth pass, one jot or one tittle shall in no wise pass from the law, till all be fulfilled" (Matthew 5:18).

We can ask immediately by what means the Christian church in the first centuries of its existence concluded that it could change the letter and the spirit of the fourth commandment. Protestants claim that the change of the Sabbath to Sunday dates back to Jesus Himself and to the apostles as a memorial of the Resurrection. On the other hand, Catholics affirm that the change was made by the sole authority of the church: "You may read the Bible from Genesis to Revelation," wrote James Cardinal Gibbons quite correctly, "and you will not find a single line authorizing the sanctification of Sunday. The Scriptures enforce the religious observance of Saturday, a day which we never sanctify" (*The Faith of Our Fathers*, 92nd edition, revised, p. 89).

The real reason for the change is found in the very nature of the fourth commandment. "The seal of God's law is found in the fourth commandment. This only, of all the ten, brings to view both the name and the title of the Lawgiver. It declares Him to be the Creator of the heavens and the earth, and thus shows His claim to reverance and worship above all others. Aside from this precept, there is nothing in the Decalogue to show by whose authority the law is given. When the Sabbath was changed by the papal power, the seal was taken from the law. The disciples of Jesus are called upon to restore it by exalting the Sabbath of the fourth commandment to its rightful position as the Creator's memorial and the sign of His authority" (*The Great Controversy*, p. 452).

This explains why the adversary has directed his attacks especially against the fourth commandment. Because the Sabbath is the memorial of creation, keeping it constitutes the sign of faithfulness to God. Worshiping God on this day truly acknowledges Him as the Creator, as opposed to all the false gods. Precisely for these reasons the Lord requires that the Sabbath be restored by those who, in the time of the end, "keep the commandments of God, and the faith of Jesus." At the time when Sunday is destined to become the mark of those who "worship the beast and his image," the Sabbath becomes once more the distinctive sign of those who worship the only true God.

On hearing this third angel's message, many will cry "legalism"—as if keeping Sunday by compulsion were not legalism. What is legalism if not the minute observation of the law in order to earn salvation? We believe that we have taken a clear stand against everything that is not salvation by grace, by means of faith. But there exists another form of legalism spoken of quite rarely: that of the scribes and Pharisees, which Jesus did not hesitate to condemn. Now, what was it that Jesus reproached them for, among other things? For tampering with the law of God, robbing it of its requirements, looking for ways to escape from it. "Ye reject the commandment of God, that ye may keep your own tradition" (Mark 7:9). When customs are no longer as high a standard as morals, then morals are lowered to the level of customs.

Replacing the law of God, which is absolute in its requirements, with substitute laws of convenience is certainly one form of legalism, for by reducing standards so that the law can be kept we produce the illusion that we are keeping the law. And from then on, like all self-righteous people, we can think that we are living in harmony with God, whereas we are only keeping a moral code made by ourselves in harmony with our own standards. No wonder Jesus specified to His disciples: "Except your righteousness shall exceed the righteousness of the scribes and Pharisees, ye shall in no case enter into the kingdom of heaven" (Matthew 5:20).

In His Sermon on the Mount Jesus declared what each disciple should know respecting the law and its observation. First, Jesus specified that He had not come to abolish the law and the prophets but to fulfill them. Then, He solemnly afffirmed that the law would remain unchanged as long as heaven and earth remain. Finally, he who would keep the law and the prophets after His example and would teach them to be binding was promised the kingdom of heaven (Matthew 5:17-19).

This is also what the third angel's message teaches us when it warns against every false worship and calls upon Christians in these last days to keep "the commandments of God, and the faith of Jesus." Today it is still possible to take a stand on behalf of the truth as it is proclaimed by the threefold message of Revelation 14. There is time still to learn how to live, by the grace of God, a life in conformity with the everlasting gospel. Tomorrow, perhaps, it will be too late, for He "that shall come will come" (Hebrews 10:37) soon, and His reward will be with Him "to give every man according as his work shall be" (22:12).

"Not every one that saith unto me, Lord, Lord, shall enter into the kingdom of heaven; but he that doeth the will of my Father which is in heaven" (Matthew 7:21).

Chapter 13

Lo! He Comes

The Christian view of history that comes to us from the Book of Revelation is, first of all, a vision of the resurrected Christ, to whom "all power is given . . . in heaven and in earth" (Matthew 28:18) and who is seated with His "Father in his throne" (3:21; compare 5:6; 1 Peter 3:22). Then follows a description of the Son of man's work—unseen, but certain and irresistible—in the affairs of this world to direct them to the goal determined by God. Everything in the Revelation converges toward this ultimate point of history: the glorious return of Christ as King of kings (1:7; 17:14; 19:16).

This triumphal coming of the Lord of history is the very theme of Revelation. Each chain of prophecy leads to this final scene, and the book itself culminates in the author's fervent prayer: "Amen. Even so, come, Lord Jesus" (22:20). For the prophet of Patmos this is not mere eschatological speculation. It would not even be correct to say that he was simply echoing the hope of the early church. John personally expected the return of Jesus, and this assurance was based directly on Jesus' promises.

In his Gospel, John took care to recall the Master's promise, made in the upper room on the eve of His parting. "Let not your heart be troubled: ye believe in God, believe also in me. In my Father's house are many mansions: if it were not so, I would have told you. I go to prepare a place for you. And if I go and prepare a place for you, I will come again, and receive you unto myself; that where I am, there ye may be also" (John 14:1-3).

Certainly John's hope was also the hope of the Apostolic Church. The hope of Jesus' return was, with faith in salvation through Christ, the main topic of the apostolic sermons and writings. There are more than three hundred references to the return of Jesus in the New Testament, without counting the numerous indirect allusions. It was not an occasional doctrine but rather an essential revelation.

As Cardinal L. Billot has very well stated: "In fact it is sufficient to turn the pages of the gospel only a very little to realize immediately that the Advent is most certainly the alpha and omega, the beginning and the end, the first and the last word of the teaching of Jesus; that it is the key, the climax, the explanation, the justification, the basis, that ultimately it is the supreme event to which all the rest is linked, and without which all the rest collapses and disappears" (*La Parousie,* pp. 9, 10).

It is not surprising, therefore, that John put the announcement of this supreme historical event in first place in the Revelation: "Behold, he cometh with clouds; and every eye shall see him, and they also which pierced him: and all kindreds of the earth shall wail because of him" (1:7).

This solemn declaration not only expresses the blessed hope of the Christian, but it also recalls the hope of the Old Testament prophets and the children of Israel. In fact, Enoch, "the seventh from Adam," had already prophesied in these words: "Behold, the Lord cometh with ten thousands of his saints, to execute judgment upon all" (Jude 14, 15).

The psalmist, too, sang of the Lord's coming: "Our God shall come, and shall not keep silence: a fire shall devour before him, and it shall be very tempestuous round about him" (Psalm 50:3).

"Let the heavens rejoice, and let the earth be glad; let the sea roar, and the fulness thereof. Let the field be joyful, and all that is therein: then shall all the trees of the wood rejoice before the Lord: for he cometh, for he cometh to judge the earth: he shall judge the world with righteousness, and the people with his truth" (Psalm 96:11-13).

"Behold, the Lord God will come with strong hand," declared the prophet Isaiah, "behold, his reward is with him, and his work before him" (Isaiah 40:10). "Behold, thy salvation cometh" (Isaiah 62:11). "For, behold, the Lord will come with fire, and with his chariots like a whirlwind" (Isaiah 66:15). The prophet Daniel's words obviously inspired John. Daniel 7:13 says, "Behold, one like the Son of man came with the clouds of heaven."

Following the example of the Old Testament prophets, John also introduced the proclamation of Jesus' coming in glory with the word *behold*. "Behold, I come quickly" (22:7, 12). "Behold, I come as a thief" (16:15). "Behold, he cometh with clouds" (1:7; compare 14:14). Obviously the sacred writers used this word to draw the attention of the reader to the declaration that followed.

Also impressive in these various statements referring to the return of Jesus is the systematic use of the present tense: "Behold, I come . . ." or "Behold, he comes. . . ." Some scholars see in this present tense a statement of Christ's continuous action in world history to establish His kingdom, from His exaltation at the right hand of God's throne until His return in the clouds of heaven. The coming of Jesus would thus be a progressive action, a historic development, an event in the process of being realized. The final episode would be His sudden appearance from high heaven at the end of time.

To the extent that the final episode is not purely and simply ignored—which is becoming more and more the case—we can certainly say that the Lord's coming has been on the way since He ascended. But stated as it is here, "Behold, he comes" indicates the certainty of His coming as well as its nearness. Furthermore, John talks of the Lord's coming "with clouds," which leaves no doubt as to the nature of the proclaimed event.

In the Bible, clouds symbolize the revelation of God's glory: "Behold, the glory of the Lord appeared in the cloud" (Exodus 16:10). Clouds are also the symbol of God's presence: "Lo, I come unto thee in a thick cloud" (Exodus 19:9; compare Numbers 11:25). Biblical examples abound. It will suffice to recall those of the Transfiguration and the Ascension. It was in the midst of a cloud that God made His voice heard (Matthew 17:5), and it was a cloud that hid Jesus from the disciples' sight (Acts 1:9).

And while the apostles looked toward heaven, they heard these words: "This same Jesus, which is taken up from you into heaven, shall so come in like manner as ye have seen him go into heaven" (verse 11). That is to say, on the clouds and in view of all. "Every eye shall see him," Revelation specifies (1:7). The event will be universal and universally seen. For as Jesus explained, "As the lightning cometh out of the east, and shineth even unto the west; so shall also the coming of the Son of man be" (Matthew 24:27).

"They also which pierced him" (1:7) will see Jesus come back in the clouds. Those who condemned Christ to the cross will have the proof that He is Christ the Son of God. "Nevertheless I say unto you," Jesus added to His judges, "hereafter shall ye see the Son of man sitting on the right hand of power, and coming in the clouds of heaven" (Matthew 26:64).

The proof will be shown, but how bitter the discovery for all those who refuse to believe that Jesus is "the Christ, the Son of the living God" (Matthew 16:16) or who wish to remain ignorant of the inevitable confrontation in the day of "the glorious appearing of the great God and our Saviour Jesus Christ" (Titus 2:13)! Then "there shall be weeping and gnashing of teeth" (Matthew 24:51; compare 13:42; 22:13; 25:30). "And then shall all the tribes of the earth mourn, and they shall see the Son of man coming in the clouds of heaven with power and great glory" (Matthew 24:30). John repeated this verse almost word for word: "And all kindreds of the earth shall wail because of him" (1:7).

At the close of the vision of the seven seals, John saw the anguish of all those who in unbelief rejected the One whom God had sent for their salvation. "And the kings of the earth, and the great men, and the rich men, and the chief captains, and the mighty men, and every bondman, and every free man, hid themselves in the dens and the rocks of the mountains; and said to the mountains and rocks, Fall on us, and hide us from the face of him that sitteth on the throne, and from the wrath of the Lamb: for the great day of his wrath is come; and who shall be able to stand?" (6:15-17).

Their question is fundamental. Who will be able to stand when the Son of God returns in the clouds of heaven? Twice the Revelation answers with the particulars. In chapter 7 we read that those clothed in white robes "are they which came out of great tribulation, and have washed their robes, and made them white in the blood of the Lamb. Therefore are they before the throne of God, and serve him day and night in his temple" (verses 14, 15). Chapter 14 calls those who have responded to the three angels' messages the "redeemed from the earth" (verse 3). "These were redeemed from among men, being the firstfruits unto God and to the Lamb. And in their mouth was found no guile: for they are without fault" (verses 4, 5).

In the first case we are dealing with the great multitude of the redeemed, "which no man could number, of all nations, and kindreds, and people, and tongues" (7:9). They bear in their foreheads "the seal of the living God" (7:2). In the second case it is more particularly a question of those who have not worshiped the beast and his image and who have not received "his mark upon their foreheads, or in their hands" (see 20:4; 14:9).

The return of Jesus as it is proclaimed in the beginning of the book deals essentially with the "how" of the event. John stressed its supernatural and universal character. Jesus will appear in the heavens "with clouds; and every eye shall see him." The second vision of Jesus' coming deals with the "why" of the event. The scene immediately follows the three angels' messages of Revelation 14 and includes a harvest of both grain and grapes.

"And I looked, and behold a white cloud, and upon the cloud one sat like unto the Son of man, having on his head a golden crown, and in his hand a sharp sickle. And another angel came out of the temple, crying with a loud voice to him that sat on the cloud, Thrust in thy sickle, and reap: for the time is come for thee to reap; for the harvest of the earth is ripe. And he that sat on the cloud thrust in his sickle on the earth; and the earth was reaped.

"And another angel came out of the temple which is in heaven, he also having a sharp sickle. And another angel

came out from the altar . . . and cried with a loud cry to him
that had the sharp sickle, saying, Thrust in thy sharp sickle,
and gather the clusters of the vine of the earth; for her
grapes are fully ripe. And the angel thrust in his sickle into
the earth, and gathered the vine of the earth, and cast it into
the great winepress of the wrath of God" (14:14-19).

Both cases deal assuredly with the coming of Jesus the
King. The aim of His coming is clearly stated: He comes,
first, to harvest the grain and, then, to gather the grapes.
The two symbols are highly suggestive of what will take
place first at the return of Christ and then when the Lord
will come to execute judgment on the wicked.

Jesus Himself explained in the parable of the tares what
the harvest signified. "The harvest is the end of the world"
(Matthew 13:39). Then the lord of the harvest "will say to
the reapers, Gather ye together first the tares, and bind
them in bundles to burn them: but gather the wheat into
my barn" (verse 30). In other words, at the time of the
world's harvest, the Lord will separate the wheat and the
tares. All those who do iniquity shall be cast "into a furnace
of fire: there shall be wailing and gnashing of teeth." In
contrast, "then shall the righteous shine forth as the sun in
the kingdom of their Father" (13:41-43).

The meaning of the grape harvest does not present any
greater difficulty, since the text refers directly to the judgment. The clusters of the vine being ripe, they are cut and
thrown "into the great winepress of the wrath of God"
(14:19). It is certainly difficult to imagine the scene described here, although the particulars given make one
tremble with horror. From all accounts it describes a final
judgment that leaves no hope of a universal salvation.

Paul left no room for doubt when he wrote: "Be not
deceived; God is not mocked: for whatsoever a man soweth, that shall he also reap. For he that soweth to his flesh
shall of the flesh reap corruption; but he that soweth to the
Spirit shall of the Spirit reap life everlasting. And let us not
be weary in well doing: for in due season we shall reap, if
we faint not" (Galatians 6:7-9).

John's third vision of Christ's coming in power and
glory revealed the Son of man as a conqueror at the head of

His army, in the fashion of the triumphal parades of the Roman emperors: "And I saw heaven opened, and behold a white horse; and he that sat upon him was called Faithful and True, and in righteousness he doth judge and make war. His eyes were as a flame of fire, and on his head were many crowns; and he had a name written, that no man knew, but he himself. And he was clothed with a vesture dipped in blood: and his name is called The Word of God. And the armies which were in heaven followed him upon white horses, clothed in fine linen, white and clean. And out of his mouth goeth a sharp sword, that with it he should smite the nations: and he shall rule them with a rod of iron: and he treadeth the winepress of the fierceness and wrath of Almighty God. And he hath on his vesture and on his thigh a name written, King of kings, and Lord of lords" (19:11-16).

For the triumph of Christ the King, the whole heavens open to make way for the passage of the Conqueror on the white horse. He who rides it is Faithfulness incarnate, Truth lived, and Justice personified. Nothing can escape His eyes of flame. The tokens of His universal royalty shine with many crowns. No one yet knows the name that is linked with "his strange work" (Isaiah 28:21), which He must do as the avenger of God's people.

And why is His vesture dipped in blood? "I have trodden the winepress alone; and of the people there was none with me: for I will tread them in mine anger, and trample them in my fury; and their blood shall be sprinkled upon my garments, and I will stain all my raiment. For the day of vengeance is in mine heart, and the year of my redeemed is come" (Isaiah 63:3, 4).

However, whether as Creator, as Saviour, or as Executor of God's justice against the rebellious world, He is still and always will be "The Word of God" (19:13). "The sharp sword" that He wields and with which He smites the nations is the Divine Word, "the sword of the Spirit" (Ephesians 6:17). It is the only weapon Christ has ever used in His warfare against evil. And by it He will cleanse the world of all pride, all lies, and all iniquity.

For this purpose God has given Him "all power . . . in

heaven and in earth" (Matthew 28:18) so "that at the name of Jesus every knee should bow, of things in heaven, and things in earth, and things under the earth; and that every tongue should confess that Jesus Christ is Lord, to the glory of God the Father" (Philippians 2:10, 11). "For he must reign, till he hath put all enemies under his feet. The last enemy that shall be destroyed is death. . . . And when all things shall be subdued unto him, then shall the Son also himself be subject unto him that put all things under him, that God may be all in all" (1 Corinthians 15:25-28).

All the visions of Revelation lead inevitably toward that grand day when "the Lord himself shall descend from heaven with a shout, with the voice of the archangel, and with the trump of God: and the dead in Christ shall rise first: then we which are alive and remain shall be caught up together with them in the clouds, to meet the Lord in the air: and so shall we ever be with the Lord" (1 Thessalonians 4:16, 17).

In the upper room during the Last Supper, Jesus had promised that He would return. On the Mount of Olives angels renewed the promise. In turn, the apostles proclaimed to the world the blessed hope of the soon return of their Saviour. And the Christians of the Apostolic Church greeted each other with the word *Maranatha,* "Our Lord, cometh" (1 Corinthians 16:22, margin). Never throughout the first century did the expectation of the Lord's coming weaken. But in order to keep it living until the return itself, the Lord made its supreme revelation to the prophet of Patmos.

The theme of the Lord's coming thrusts itself forward with extraordinary power in the Revelation. From the first verses until the last words of the book, the promise of His return sounds forth from nearly every page. Its surety and its imminence are constantly reaffirmed. All the things revealed to John would "shortly come to pass" (1:1), "for the time is at hand" (1:3). "Behold, he cometh" (1:7).

In His letters to the seven churches, Jesus spoke unceasingly of His coming. To the Thyatira Christians, He said, "I will put upon you none other burden. But that which ye have already hold fast till I come" (2:24, 25). To the church at

Sardis, He warned: "If therefore thou shalt not watch, I will come on thee as a thief, and thou shalt not know what hour I will come upon thee" (3:3). To the church at Philadelphia, He announced His soon coming: "Behold, I come quickly: hold that fast which thou hast, that no man take thy crown" (3:11). To Laodicea, finally, He specified that He was "at the door" (3:20).

At the end of the vision of the seven trumpets John wrote: "There were great voices in heaven, saying, The kingdoms of this world are become the kingdoms of our Lord, and of his Christ; and he shall reign for ever and ever" (11:15). In the vision depicting the eve of the battle of Armageddon, the Lord repeated His promise once more: "Behold, I come as a thief. Blessed is he that watcheth, and keepeth his garments, lest he walk naked, and they see his shame" (16:15).

At the very end of the book the Lord repeated the promise three times. "Behold, I come quickly: blessed is he that keepeth the sayings of the prophecy of this book. . . . For the time is at hand" (22:7, 10).

A second time the Lord took up the same message: "And, behold, I come quickly; and my reward is with me, to give every man according as his work shall be. I am Alpha and Omega, the beginning and the end, the first and the last. Blessed are they that do his commandments, that they may have right to the tree of life, and may enter in through the gates into the city" (22:12-14).

Finally, at the end of this series of prophetic appeals comes the last declaration of Jesus, putting as it were a final note not only on the Revelation but on the entire Bible: "He which testifieth these things saith, Surely I come quickly" (22:20).

"And the Spirit and the bride say, Come. And let him that heareth say, Come" (22:17). And the prophet of Patmos took the words out of the Lord's mouth and addressed this final prayer to Him:

"Amen. Even so, come, Lord Jesus" (22:20).